A LITTLE CHILD
SHALL LEAD THEM

NOEL DAVIDSON

AMBASSADOR INTERNATIONAL
Greenville, South Carolina • Belfast, Northern Ireland

A LITTLE CHILD SHALL LEAD THEM
© Copyright 2005 Noel Davidson

ISBN 1 84030 159 7

Ambassador Publications
a division of
Ambassador Productions Ltd.
Providence House
Ardenlee Street,
Belfast,
BT6 8QJ
Northern Ireland
www.ambassador-productions.com

Ambassador International
427 Wade Hampton Blvd.
Greenville
SC 29609, USA

CONTENTS

INTRODUCTION

John had a problem. He had begun to write a biography and had so many experiences to recount and conversations to record that he was almost overwhelmed. In fact when he came to the end of his book he said that if he had been able to portray all that his subject had done it would be doubtful if the world could hold all the books he would have to write.

It was a question of selection. John had been a close companion of the only Perfect Man who ever graced this planet and his mind was awash with precious memories. In the end he needed the guidance of the Spirit of God to help him choose the most suitable incidents and most significant utterances to describe for us.

On the afternoon I first met Trevor and Esther Gillanders, just over a year ago, it was with the view to writing an article on their experiences for Life Times, a Christian magazine.

They told me the story of their little son Raymond, or 'wee Monty' as they called him affectionately, and showed me a lovely photograph of him in their lounge. As the story unfolded I learnt that Raymond had been born with Down's syndrome and an incurable heart condition. Caring for him had afforded them much joy, parting with him after seventeen months gave them great sorrow and presented them with the challenge of life, death and the big beyond.

How they both became Christians some time after Raymond's unexpected death took another page in my notebook. When they went on to recollect how they had gone to Bible College, and then into full time evangelism with The Faith Mission, I was fascinated, touched and often amused.

As they proceeded to relate to me incident after incident of God's wonderful working in their lives and ministry I realised that I, too, was going to have a problem with selection. And still they were rattling on. 'We mustn't forget to tell you about what happened in Cork...or Coagh...or Castleblayney...'

By the time I came to the last question I had prepared for that interview, I had quietly closed my notebook. The question was, "And how did you come to be in Larne?" and I asked it anyway.

"Oh that's a story all on it's own," was Trevor's immediate reply.

So had they all been, though. Raymond, their separate conversions, their years at Bible College, the unbelievable blessing in some of their missions, the camp centre in Cork, the provision for their home in Monaghan... they were every one 'stories all on their own!'

"There is no way that I could do justice to all that you have told me in a magazine article," I said, placing my pen back in my pocket. "I would never be able to decide what to put in, but I wouldn't dare leave anything out. This isn't a magazine article. This is a book! If you don't mind, I will be in touch with my publishers and see what they think."

When I did as I had suggested, and contacted Ambassador, they must have sensed my enthusiasm for such a project, and my admiration for the two humble servants of the Lord involved, for they gave their consent to it almost immediately.

It has been a pleasure to work with Trevor and Esther for the last twelve months or so, for they are such open, friendly and sincere Christian people. A 'Lovely Couple,' as I have to take a whole chapter to tell you! I might also say that it has been unusually convenient to work with them for it takes me less than five minutes to drive from my front door to theirs!

We have gone through the whole gamut of emotions together when writing this book. On the day we were speaking of how 'wee Monty,' passed away Esther dropped a silent tear. "Don't worry if I get a bit emotional this morning, Noel," she said. "This is bringing it all back."

On other occasions we laughed heartily together, like the time Trevor began to tell how pots and pots of lovely home-made jam flooded into the mission in Garvagh.

This book recounts both sad and amusing incidents, but it is, in essence, a testimony to the power of God, both to draw people to Himself in a wonderful way, and to provide for His children in an equally miraculous manner.

There would be no story at all though, if there hadn't been one little Down's syndrome boy, who was often ill, but who dispensed so much joy in his short lifetime. That was 'our wee Monty.'

At his funeral, the minister quoted the words from the Bible, 'a little child shall lead them', and that was to prove prophetic. For following his death his mum and dad were led to faith in Christ, and through them his two brothers, Darren and Gregory, and after that hundreds more besides.

Trevor, Esther and I, and indeed all involved in the writing and publication of this book, pray that it will introduce a new phase to that ministry. We long to learn of the 'little child' of the title having led many of its readers to faith in Christ, and onward into a life of fruitful service for Him.

Noel Davidson
March 2005

Other books by the same author

MY FATHER'S HAND

THIS IS FOR REAL

JUST THE WAY I AM

SOME PARTY IN HEAVEN

FIRST CITIZEN SMYTH

SOMETHING WORTH LIVING FOR

HOW SWEET THE SOUND

AS OUR HEADS ARE BOWED

ONLY THE BEST WILL DO

A BRUISED REED

BACK FROM THE BRINK

OUT OF THE MAZE

THE TANGLED LAMB

SOLDIER, SAILOR, LIVE OR DIE

I BELIEVE GOD

PAINTING THE TOWN RED

WHO CARES?

SIGN OF THE FISH

OUT OF THE DEEP

NOT BY MIGHT

1

HOW DID YOU KNOW, ESTHER?

"I'm telling you, Trevor. There is definitely something wrong with this baby," Esther Gillanders insisted to her husband as they walked across to their car, which was parked outside Monaghan General Hospital.

It was April 1981, and Esther, who was expecting the couple's second child, had just emerged from one of her regular check-ups at the pre-natal clinic. Trevor and Esther already had a little two-year old son, Darren, and he was due to be joined by a baby brother or sister in a few months time.

"Why do you always keep saying that, Esther?" her husband wanted to know. "Did they tell you that in there?"

"No. They didn't. They say everything's normal. Just fine. But I know it isn't," came the emphatic reply.

"Well you would think the doctors and nurses would probably know what they are talking about," Trevor went on, trying to allay his own sneaking reservations about his wife's pessimistic, but purely personal, prognosis. "And if they are happy that the baby is O.K. how on earth can you say that you know it isn't?"

"I wish you would stop asking me how I know, Trevor," Esther told him, beginning to sound just mildly irritated by her husband's persistence. This strange feeling that had beset her, almost from the start of the pregnancy, was upsetting for her, too, and Trevor's understandable concern did nothing to help untangle her mixed-up emotions.

"I don't know how I know. But I just know, if that makes any sense to you," she declared categorically. "Now can we leave it there?"

The pair had just reached the car, and as they prepared to move off Trevor agreed not to talk about it any more that day.

He was well aware, though, that the subject would come up again, as it had done, a number of times already. There had been conversations like this before, usually initiated by his wife. They were most liable to occur at night, after they had looked in on their soundly sleeping two-year old, climbed into bed, and switched out the light.

That seemed to be Esther's favourite time to share her inexplicable premonition by whispering, "I'm sure there is something the matter with this baby I'm going have."

"A lot of nonsense, Esther," had been her husband's initial stock reply to such assertions. This was spoken with no hint of hardness, but in an effort to dampen his wife's over-active imagination, and help her see what he called 'reason.' "You will see. Everything will be all right. Time will tell."

"That's right, Trevor. Time will tell. But it will probably be you who will see," was the expectant mother's continual response to such attempted reassurances.

This conflict of Esther's basic maternal instinct and her husband's manly common sense fuelled by an underlying unwillingness to accept the implications of her prediction, surfaced at least once every two or three weeks for the next four months.

That took them up to mid-August when Esther was admitted to the maternity ward of Monaghan General Hospital to have her second child.

When the baby was eventually born, on August 19, after a

protracted labour, he was blue. This caused a flurry of activity among the medical staff around the bed, and in the midst of all the hustle and bustle someone remarked to Esther, "You'll be pleased to know it's a boy."

The staff, who were preparing to give the baby life-saving treatment, were shocked at the mother's instinctive outburst in response to the announcement of the birth of her second son.

"Take him away!" she exclaimed. "Take him away! I don't want to see him!"

This highly unusual explosion of emotion came as a total surprise to a senior midwife. "Why do you not want to see your baby?" she enquired, almost involuntarily.

"He's a mongol," Esther replied with an air of authority, but unaware of the more acceptable description of the condition, until corrected by a member of the nursing staff, who overheard her outburst..

The midwife who had asked the question had no answer to that pronouncement. She just shrugged her shoulders, turned her back and left to help attend to the urgent needs of the baby. The child had only been born a matter of minutes and the medical staff were too busy trying to keep him alive to have carried out any kind of examination or assessment. Who was this half-hysterical mother to say something like that, she must have wondered. She would probably dismiss the incident by attributing her abnormal attitude to the trauma of the birth.

A junior nurse had been sitting at Esther's side, holding the new mother's hand during and after the birth, and she too had heard all the strange things that she had said. Her immediate reaction, though, was completely different to that of anyone Esther had ever spoken to about her premonition, including her husband.

Although she couldn't, at that stage, have known anything about the baby's condition, this nurse leaned over and whispered softly into her ear, "How did you know, Esther?"

Alerted by a sense of understanding in another human being, the almost distraught mother looked across at the sympathetic young woman beside her, and whispered back, "God told me."

This was a totally untypical response from Esther.

She had been brought up in the Church of Ireland, but since marrying Trevor she had joined him in membership of his home church, which was Ballyalbany Presbyterian, in Monaghan. They were members, though, and nothing more. Church was, for them, a necessary institution for the conduct of weddings and funerals, and a useful place to go for a shot of the feel-good factor at Christmas and Easter, but that was all.

Trevor was a baker and worked long, and often unsociable, hours, and when he and his wife did have time to go out for an evening it was usually to a dance, not a church service.

Esther had shown, up until then, little more than a passing interest in the Almighty, her sole connection with God having been a formal, and not terribly interested, attendance at church during her teenage years. Now she claimed that it was God who had told her that something was amiss with her baby!

It was reassuring to have somebody beside her, to listen. The junior nurse may have found her claim to divine revelation just as peculiar as the midwife had found her declaration of disinterest, but she didn't say so. The anxious mother wasn't, for once, greeted with, 'Have a bit of sense, Esther,' or, 'A load of nonsense, Esther,' or, 'It's just your imagination, Esther.'

The young nurse's only response was to smile kindly and say softly, "Oh, is that right?"

Just over an hour later, when Esther had calmed down a little emotionally, and was feeling just slightly more comfortable physically, the ward sister came to sit on the edge of her bed.

Having asked her patient a number of questions about her condition the sister went on to say, "Your little baby is lovely, Esther. We have him in an incubator in the nursery and he is doing well."

"That's good," Esther replied. "But you know that I don't want him."

The sister, pretending to sound shocked, replied, "Surely you must want your own little baby. And if you don't want him, what are we going to do with him?"

"I don't know what you will do with him, but that is really your problem," the adamant mother went on, not just as loudly, but every bit as firmly, as before.

There was silence for a second or two. The sister needed time to think that one through, before replying, but before she could utter a word, Esther was in again.

"I tell you one thing I would like you to do for me, if you really want to help me. Go and get me my son Darren's photograph out of the bag I brought in with me," she said. "I want to put it up on my locker."

"No, Esther. That's not fair. You can't make a difference..." the sister began, trying to appeal to an unusually headstrong mother's temporarily dormant maternal instinct.

She didn't have time to finish her sentence. Esther interrupted her by announcing, " Well, if you won't go for it for me, then I will get it myself!" and with that she threw down the covers and turned as though to slide out of the bed.

"No! Don't do that! I will find the photo for you!" This time it was the sister's turn to interrupt. When she had seen her patient settled back into the bed she complied with Esther's request and brought her the photograph of her first little son.

She looked at it intently for almost a minute before reaching over to prop it up on her locker. Although still desperately weak, and thoroughly upset, Esther afforded herself the hint of a smile as she thought about Darren. He had brought Trevor and her so much pleasure over the previous two years.

What, though, was to become of the tiny baby in the nursery?

Was there 'something wrong with him,' as Esther had always maintained?

And more importantly, who was going to look after him if his mother refused to?

2

WHERE'S TREVOR?

While all this high drama was unfolding up in Monaghan General Hospital, Trevor, husband of the uptight mother, and father of the newly-born baby which she claimed she didn't want, was at home, in bed, asleep.

The anxious father had gone up to the hospital just before midnight but the staff had told him that he wasn't allowed to go in. "We think you should go home to bed," they had advised. "Nothing is going to happen here tonight."

That was just before things really did begin to happen.

Suddenly, around 4.00 a.m. he awoke with a start and instantly, instinctively, jumped out of bed.

Something was wrong. He just knew it.

It was as though some sixth sense had alerted him to the plight of his wife.

He had to find out what was happening, but rather than turn up at the hospital to be turned away again, he decided to phone before going up. That wasn't just as easy as it could have been, however, for Trevor and Esther didn't have a telephone.

Darren was away staying with an aunt so at least he didn't have to worry about him. Having pulled on a pair of trousers and a sweater he then slipped on a pair of shoes before rushing out the front. There was a public telephone down at the end of the street and there was hardly likely to be a queue for it at ten past four in the morning.

Trevor didn't reach the telephone kiosk, though.

He didn't need to.

As he was hurrying down the street he met his brother Leary coming up.

The two brothers were amazed to meet each other, running in opposite directions in the middle of the night. When they stopped, Trevor noticed a look of concern on his brother's face and after they had taken a few seconds to recover enough breath to say anything, Leary gasped out his message.

"The hospital have just been on the phone, Trevor," he said. "You are to get up there as soon as possible. There's something wrong. Esther is all right, but there's something wrong with the baby."

Trevor was seized with a blind panic. He turned on his heel, and without saying, or waiting to hear, anything else he dashed back up to the house. He had his car keys in his pocket and so he jumped into the car and raced wildly up to the hospital, not knowing what he was going to find there.

He was not turned at the door this time, but met instead by a senior midwife who talked to him as they walked quickly along the corridor.

"We are really worried about your wife, Esther," she explained. "She is very distressed. In fact she appears almost hysterical at times. She keeps asking, 'Where's Trevor? Where's Trevor?' I'm glad to see you here. Hopefully you will be able to help us calm her down."

"I hope I will," the anxious husband replied, striding out purposefully. All that mattered to him now was reaching her as soon as possible. At that point he would have been the first to confess he could do with some calming down himself.

When the midwife led him to where Esther was, he burst into the small side-ward and was confronted with the pathetic sight of his distraught wife. It almost broke his heart. He stepped across to the side of the bed and immediately took her hand in his.

"Oh Trevor, I'm glad to see you!" Esther cried out at once, and then went on, "Our baby is Downs. That's what I told you! That's what I have been telling everybody for months but nobody believed me!"

"It will be all right," Trevor replied softly, not knowing how best to reply to this declaration of the truth of his wife's long-held premonition. "Don't worry."

"How can I not worry, Trevor?" came back the almost hysterical response from the bed. "The nurses say that we will soon be able to take him home, but I don't want to take him home. How could I ever manage to look after him? He would need a lot more attention than Darren did as a baby, you know."

Trevor sat beside the bed, still holding Esther's hand and speaking gently to her. He responded to all her observations, a number of which were sensible enough but others were frenzied and unreasonable, and he answered all her questions as best he could.

It took time, but at last Esther seemed to become less agitated. She usually found her husband's apparently cool, calm and collected approach to most matters had a settling influence on her, and she had rarely needed it more than she did that night.

Although adopting a seemingly strong and serene stance in the situation, Trevor had his reservations too. He secretly shared some of his wife's concerns about the issues that were causing her such distress, but he knew that he daren't voice these, at least not at that particular time.

When he had been in with Esther for more than an hour, and was satisfied that she was now sufficiently settled to do without him for a short time Trevor said to her, "You will be O.K. there for a minute or two, won't you, if I go to the nursery to see our new baby."

Esther nodded. She would be fine for a while. He could go to the nursery if he liked as long as he didn't expect her to go with him.

On arriving outside the nursery to try and see the latest addition to their family he looked in through the large glass window. When he did this he discovered that there were a number of babies in there. They were all in small cots except for one which was in an incubator.

As he wasn't allowed to enter the nursery without the permission of the duty nurse, Trevor continued to stand outside gazing in through the glass partition.

When the nurse spotted him there she waved for him to come in, and as she already knew him, merely smiled and said, "Over here."

Trevor followed her dutifully, and when she came to the incubator she opened it, reached in carefully, and then turning reached the tiny baby boy to its proud father.

"Would you like to hold him a minute?" she enquired.

"I would indeed," Trevor replied, and took the little bundle of humanity in his arms. He stood there cradling him in his arm, amazed at the perfection of his little body. Trevor recognised, at that instant, that this was his second precious son, and vowed that he would be every bit as much loved as the first. The inner turmoil and secret misgivings had gone. They had evaporated the minute he had taken the little one into his arms.

If only Esther could see him, he thought, she would love him just as much as me.

He continued to feast his eyes on his second little son until the nurse came to return him to the incubator. It was hard to tear himself away from the baby but he knew that he had to describe to Esther what he had just seen. The picture of a little baby, who appeared absolutely perfect to him, regardless of what his wife or anybody else said, was etched indelibly on his mind.

Trevor turned round to go, and then turned back to have another look, twice, before eventually setting off across the corridor to where Esther lay in the side ward. He had such wonderful news for his wife.

Esther was lying back on the pillow with her eyes closed when he arrived back at her bedside. He paused a moment before speaking, but when she began to stir in the bed he burst out enthusiastically, "I don't know what you are worried about, Esther. I have just seen our baby in the nursery and he is absolutely gorgeous! He is in an incubator, mind you, but the nurse lifted him out and let me hold him. He has ginger hair and you want to see his wee hands. They are just perfect. If you could only see him..."

He stopped suddenly, mid-sentence. Esther had closed her eyes again. He had the impression that his wife either didn't hear what he was saying or didn't want to hear what he was saying. There were, though, two things which he didn't fully appreciate.

The first of these was how physically weak and ill his wife felt. She was completely drained after the birth. The other was even more difficult to understand, as it could not possibly be recognised by visual observation.

It was the complete and utter turmoil that was tormenting her mind.

Esther wanted to be interested in what he was saying. But she wasn't.

She was trying hard to believe what he was telling her. But she couldn't.

It was as though her mind had gone numb. Everything around her seemed so remote, and cold, and dead.

Trevor stopped talking and just sat holding her hand. The contact had a soothing effect on both of them.

It was a long time before Esther spoke, and when she did it was to make a simple request. "Sure you won't leave me here on my own, Trevor," she begged. "Promise me that you will stay with me until the morning."

That was an easy promise to make, for he had no intention of leaving Esther for a while. The hospital staff appreciated the calming effect he had been able to exert on her, so they weren't likely to ask him to leave. Anyway, it was already morning. The grey light of dawn had begun to appear through chinks in the curtains all around the building.

"Yes, Esther. I will stay with you for as long as I can," he assured her.

"I promise."

3

HE IS LOVELY!

Esther was glad to have Trevor with her for company for the next few hours. When the hospital became busier, however, with the daytime staff taking over from the night shift, and orderlies beginning to serve breakfast, Trevor knew that he would have to go.

He had a number of important matters to attend to, including telling both families, and some close friends, about the birth of their second son. Esther didn't want to let him leave but she knew that he was right. Everybody would be anxious to hear the latest news, especially since Leary had been contacted and told that 'there was something wrong with the baby.'

Trevor was on his feet, preparing to go, and they were still discussing who he should 'tell first,' when his wife remembered someone she was sure would be interested, and who she had promised to let know when 'anything happened.'

"And Trevor, make sure you let Violet know," she instructed

him.

"I will, no problem," her husband promised her, and then, having gone over his mental checklist with her once more, left the ward.

Esther lay back and thought of Violet. It was fascinating how they had come to know each other.

Violet's mum lived near Trevor's parents, and the families had become friendly. One day when Trevor and Esther had called to see Violet's mother, Violet was there and she had a baby in her arms.

"What do you call your baby?" Esther enquired.

"This is Mark," Violet replied, smiling.

"Do you mind if I hold him?" was Esther's next question.

When the obviously proud mum had handed little Mark across to Esther she sat down to nurse him. As she looked at him Esther noticed that he was Down's syndrome but that didn't in any way lessen his appeal for the mother-to-be. On the contrary, it seemed to make him more attractive. Esther kept repeating, "Isn't he just gorgeous! Isn't he just gorgeous!"

She enjoyed nursing baby Mark, but when the visit was over she returned him, somewhat reluctantly to his mum, and left.

On the day before she had gone into hospital Esther met Violet again, on the street in Monaghan.

It was at least three months since they had met in Violet's mother's home. "It's Violet, isn't it?" she began by way of introduction.

"Yes. It is," Violet replied warmly. "How are you Esther?"

Esther chose to ignore that question for she had another of her own to ask. "How's Mark?" was what she was anxious to know, when she realised that Violet didn't have him with her.

"He's fine," his mum assured her. "Why don't you call round and see him sometime?"

"I would love to, but I will have to wait until after my baby's born now," Esther told her.

Now that her baby had been born she hoped that Trevor would remember to tell Violet. She appeared so kind and caring and would no doubt identify with how Esther felt at that moment.

When breakfast was over Esther was moved out of the side ward where she had spent the night, and into a larger ward with three other women. It was good to have the company but Esther worried a bit at first about what she would say if they asked her about her baby.

She couldn't say that she hadn't had him yet, for she had.

Nor could she say that he hadn't lived, for he had.

It was going to be awkward to say that he was in an incubator in the nursery, but she had no intention of going to see him.

She would have to tell them that though, for that was the truth.

That was, of course, if they ever asked. But they didn't.

It was uncanny. Here were three women. All new mothers and all with new babies, but nobody ever asked her if she had one.

Perhaps they knew.

Esther spent a difficult morning in her new surroundings. She was trying to get over the birth of her second baby in a number of ways, and it wasn't proving easy. Physically, she was still very weak and in need of careful medical attention, but she could cope with that. It was not pleasant, but it was not unusual.

The nursing staff on the ward were concerned about her mental and emotional state. They found it strange that this new mother was still insisting that she didn't want to see her baby. Their but-thinly-veiled surprise had the knock-on effect of causing Esther to embark on a turbulent flight into self-examination. She agonised over her inability to relate to her newborn child.

What is wrong with me? she kept asking herself, over and over again. They tell me it's the most natural thing in the world for a mother to want to hold her baby close to her breast. Why do I feel so desensitised, so distant, so detached, so dead inside?

Lunch was barely over on the ward when the agitated mother had a visitor. It was Violet. Obviously Trevor had been working on his 'list of people to tell.'

There was a serenity about Violet's attitude that made Esther feel less stressed, almost at once.

She stepped across to the bed with a broad smile and greeted her with a cheery, "Hello, Esther. It's good to see you." Then, setting a small parcel, wrapped in blue paper with happy looking babies printed all over it, down on the bed at Esther's right hand, she went on, "And there's a little something for your new wee boy."

"Oh thank you, Violet," Esther said at once. "Thank you for coming to see me, and thank you for this too." She held up the parcel and then began to open it.

When she had removed the paper as carefully as possible, for it would, she thought, be a shame to rip it off in pieces, Esther exclaimed spontaneously, "Oh, isn't that just lovely!"

Inside the parcel was a little suit, folded in tissue paper. It was a beige jumper and a pair of tiny brown trousers, for a little boy.

Esther's eyes filled up with tears. She was overwhelmed. Things had all seemed to be going against her, and now a sudden chink of sunshine had penetrated her dark world. This simple act of kindness had made her begin to feel human again.

"Thank you, Violet," she repeated. "What a cute little suit! How can I thank you enough?"

The fact that a woman, whom she had only met a few months earlier, would take the time to spend the money to buy such a beautiful and useful present for her baby son had left her flabbergasted.

Violet sat down on a chair beside the bed and they began to talk.

Esther asked about Mark, and then Violet in turn enquired after Darren. Who was keeping him? How was he doing? Did he know yet that he had a baby brother?

The tension was easing. For once the new mother didn't feel under pressure in a conversation. Even when the subject of the new baby came around she was quite willing to share her feelings with her visitor.

"Have you been up to see him yet?" Violet asked.

"No, to be honest, I haven't," came Esther's ready reply. "For some reason I can't bring myself round to going to see him. You might find that difficult to understand, but it's the way I feel."

Esther wondered what Violet, who had been so kind, would say in response to this confession of an apparently unnatural reaction.

She needn't have worried.

The lady in the chair at the bedside merely smiled once more and said, "Don't worry, Esther. I do understand."

That was most comforting. Somebody at last understood.

They chatted on for another few minutes before Violet remarked, "I think I should be going soon, Esther, but would you mind if I went up to the nursery to see the baby before I go?"

"Not at all, Violet, go ahead," was Esther's immediate reply.

Violet rose to take her at her word, whispering, "I'll call in and speak to you before I go."

When Violet left to go to the nursery Esther began to reflect on her feelings once more. And they were different. She was beginning to feel at peace with herself. She wasn't quite so frazzled.

Why should this be?

There could only be one answer. It was because of Violet's approach.

Here was someone who hadn't driven her further into distraction by telling her how she should or should not feel, or what she should or should not do. She had just accepted what she had to say, with obvious understanding and not the remotest suggestion of condemnation.

Esther was still in the middle of her reverie when Violet arrived back in with her once more. It was time she was on her way home, she told the by now slightly less perplexed woman in the bed, but she had one further word of encouragement for the confused mother before she left.

Leaning across towards her, Violet said softy, "He is lovely, Esther."

4

THAT'S MY BABY!

Violet turned back once, briefly, at the door of the ward, smiled, waved, and was gone.

There was now no time to lose.

If the baby in the nursery was as 'lovely' as Violet had said he was, Esther decided that it was time she had made an effort to go to see him. Her maternal instincts had conquered her mixed-up emotions at last. Violet was barely out the hospital gate until Esther was out of bed. I'm going to the nursery to see my baby she resolved, almost in spite of herself. She pulled on her dressing gown hurriedly, shoved her feet into her slippers and was on her way.

As Esther approached the nursery her pace slackened. Would it be all right to go on in, she wondered. And how am I going to know which baby is mine anyway? What will the nurses say to me for not coming to see him long ago? All kinds of thoughts besieged her mind, but she continued to advance, although a little more slowly.

When she arrived at the large window of the nursery Esther peered in.

There were rows of tiny cots and most of them held a tiny baby. There was an incubator over near the wall with a baby in it too. Over at the other side of the ward sat a nurse with a baby on her knee. She was feeding it with a bottle.

The nurse lifted her head momentarily and glanced across at the window. When she saw Esther standing gazing in, as though in a trance, she moved the bottle into the other hand, and using the hand she had just freed up, beckoned Esther to come in. She recognised the importance of the moment, and the battle that Esther had won to bring her to that particular spot, and so she made the most of it.

As soon as the new mother opened the door and slowly, self-consciously, entered the nursery, the duty nurse made an attempt to put her at her ease.

"Come on in, Esther," she began, and then immediately burst into tears.

"What's wrong?" Esther asked anxiously. Could there possibly be something more wrong with her baby than she already knew about?

"I'm sorry about last night," the nurse explained through her tears. "You were very distressed and I thought later that I should have stayed with you instead of going off duty when my shift was over. I have felt awful about it ever since."

"Don't worry about that," Esther replied. "I never thought a thing about it."

What had happened the previous day was history to Esther now. She was walking across towards the incubator as she spoke.

On reaching it she stood motionless, staring at the little baby inside. His head was covered with fine hair, which had a distinctly reddish tinge. It glinted in the light. Despite all the tubes and wires around him he looked beautiful to his young mother. Tears trickled down her cheeks.

"Go on, Esther. Open up the incubator. You can reach in and touch him," the nurse encouraged her from the other side of the room.

Esther turned round to look in the direction of the voice only to discover that the nurse was weeping silently too. It was a big moment for both of them.

Gently, cautiously, Esther pulled open the door at the side. A tiny hand lay exposed, right at the opening. The mother, who had once said that she didn't even want to see this baby, not to mention touch him, reached in and took the little hand in hers.

Bonding had begun.

Esther stood there looking at her baby son, through her tears. The tangled emotions that had screwed her up so badly inside since he was born had all become unravelled and were flooding out.

"How will he ever forgive me?" she kept muttering to herself. "How will he ever forgive me?"

When the nurse had returned the baby she had been feeding to its cot she came over and stood slightly behind Esther. She remained there for a minute, savouring the scene. The mother had become totally engrossed with her baby.

"Would you like me to lift him out for you, Esther?" she enquired softly, at length.

"Yes, please," the conscience-stricken mother replied, her voice barely audible.

No sooner had Esther given the assent than the nurse stepped forward and opened up the incubator fully and was reaching in for the baby. Esther pulled a nearby chair up as close as she could and sat down. Then the nurse handed her little son down on to her lap.

"Oh how will he ever forgive me?" she asked again, guiltily.

"Don't worry, Esther. The important thing is that you are here now, and that you have taken him in your arms," the nurse assured her.

And she was right.

An overwhelming sense of affection gradually displaced the nagging guilt that had plagued the new mother as she had stood transfixed, a few minutes earlier, holding her baby's hand.

The initial thrill of having him on her knee for the first time intensified as she began a meticulous, awestruck examination of the tiny frame. She began with the perfect little red hands and feet, peeping out at the ends of the hospital gown. She counted the miniature fingers and toes, holding each one between finger and thumb as she did so. Then it was on to the face. His little round mouth, the minute nose, and the closed eyes were all subjected to adoring scrutiny. Esther then spent some time gazing at the silky strands of red hair that covered his head. One or two of them seemed damp, others out of place. Esther smoothed and stroked them tenderly with her hand. She looked down at the baby she thought she didn't want to see and her heart was filled with love and joy.

Bonding was complete.

When the nurse thought that it was time for the little one to be returned to the incubator she took him from his mother and placed him back carefully, making him as comfortable as possible.

Esther stood lingering over the incubator for some time before deciding that she should go back to the ward. She felt like a different person by then, however.

After visiting time later that evening, and when all the husbands had gone home, the mothers in the ward were having a chat. Their discussion centred on various aspects of one common theme, the having and raising of babies.

Esther volunteered the occasional comment but no one, as yet, had even hinted that she was a new mother like the other three of them.

Suddenly one girl said, "My husband was in the nursery this evening and he says there is the most gorgeous wee baby down there in an incubator. Have any of you seen it?"

The time had come for Esther to enter the conversation in earnest.

"Yes," she replied, with a broad smile on her face and an instant surge of pride welling up in her heart. "I have. That's my baby!"

5

THE PARTING OF THE WAYS

Life now held more hope.

The baby belonged to Trevor and Esther. They were united in the thrill of parenthood and were determined to give him all the love and attention possible, as normal parents would.

The first decision they had to make, now that Esther had come to accept the baby as her own, was to give him a name that they both liked, and that suited him. It is a choice faced by all new parents, but many have the name-game solved during the mother's pregnancy, having selected a list of possible alternatives.

Trevor and Esther hadn't done that, for Esther had been so obsessed with her premonition that there was 'something not right with it,' they had never even considered that 'it' might one day need a name. As they began, together, to consider a number that each of them liked personally, they then settled on a few that appealed to them both as a couple, and finally chose the one that best seemed to suit their new baby.

It was Raymond.

When the baby was just three days old Esther was told that she could go home but Raymond would have to remain in hospital a little longer for he had jaundice.

On the day that Esther was to leave hospital Trevor and Darren had gone out to Trevor's mum for lunch and Esther's sister Frances had come into the ward to help the new mother prepare to leave. The plan was that Frances would stay at home with Esther a few days after her discharge, as Trevor had to go to work.

It was just after lunch and Esther was in the bathroom getting dressed when the door knocked and someone called, "Can I come in?"

"Yes, certainly," Esther replied. She had recognised the voice. It was one of the nurses. She pushed the door open and sat down on the edge of the bath.

The nurse paused a moment before sharing the disturbing news she had come to deliver. "Could you sit down here beside me?" she said. "I have something I want to tell you."

Esther did as she was told, wondering what was coming next. She had spent months thinking the worst about her new baby, but that was all now in the past. There was nothing left of it but a lingering, niggling sense of remorse. Now that she had discovered she loved him so much, any bad news would be virtually unbearable.

"It's about Raymond," the nurse began. "We have to move him to another hospital for as far as we know he has a heart condition. He needs to have more intensive tests urgently, but we can't find a major hospital that will take him because he has not been christened."

"Oh no!" Esther exclaimed, bursting into floods of tears. "What next?"

The nurse sat silently with her until she had regained some measure of composure, before going on, "Could you contact your husband and have a christening arranged as soon as possible?"

In a blind panic, but impelled into action by a sense of absolute urgency, Esther found a few coins from somewhere and eventually succeeded in getting a message through to her husband from a call-box in the hospital.

Raymond was very ill, Trevor was shocked to learn, on receiving it. They wanted to send him to another hospital, but it appeared to be the policy of most hospitals that they wouldn't receive a baby as a transfer patient unless he or she had been christened. Could he sort something out as soon as possible?

It was a difficult assignment for a couple of reasons. Firstly, Trevor was overcome by an instant annoyance, verging on anger. If his little baby needed urgent medical care why were they fussing about some religious tradition or other, before giving it to him, he wanted to know. Realising that such an approach might be both natural and understandable, but it wouldn't help solve the situation in the long run, he then began to think of contacting their minister in Ballyalbany Presbyterian Church, Rev. David Hillen.

He felt bad about this for he and Esther only attended church on the rarest of special occasions. This, though, was an emergency, and since it had religious overtones, Trevor reckoned that the church minister would be his most useful point of contact.

Nothing was going to be that simple, though. When Trevor phoned the manse he was informed that Rev. Hillen was on holiday and given another number. One thing had become obvious straightaway. If Raymond were to be christened, it wouldn't be their own minister who would do it.

Trevor decided to ring him nonetheless, at the number he had been given. Perhaps he could suggest someone else who could fill in for him.

When, eventually, he heard David Hillen's voice at the other end of a telephone line he was relieved. "What's wrong, Trevor? How can I help you?" the minister was eager to know. He had assumed that there must be something quite serious the matter to inspire a man who hardly came to church during the eleven months of the year that he was in town, to phone him on his holidays.

It took Trevor a few minutes to give the minister the important facts of the position and explain the immediacy of the problem they faced. It didn't take Rev. Hillen long to sum up the situation and give his response. This, when it came, didn't seem to be entirely helpful to the anxious father in the short term, but it was ultimately reassuring.

What he said was, "You don't need to worry about having your baby christened, Trevor. It is a mere ceremony, and has no effect on present or future happiness or security. If anything happens to little Raymond he will go straight to heaven."

It was all right to say that christening wasn't necessary, but if your baby was dying and the hospital authorities wouldn't treat him without it having been done, it was a different matter, Trevor thought when he came off the phone. It was good though, to learn that 'if anything happens to him,' which was soften-the-blow speak for, 'if he dies,' he would 'go straight to heaven.'

Thinking that Esther and the hospital staff would be waiting to see what he had come up with, Trevor phoned them back and said that Rev. Hillen wasn't available. It was only then that he learnt that events had taken another dramatic turn. While he had been trying to contact his minister, it appeared that the medical staff, becoming increasingly concerned about the baby's critical condition, had continued to phone other hospitals with specialist units to see if any of them would be willing to admit him.

They had found one they said. A hospital in Drogheda would take him in as long as Esther and he would agree to allow the hospital chaplain to christen him if they considered it necessary.

Of course they would! If it was going to mean a matter of life or death for their terribly sick baby, of course they would. They would agree to anything within their power, and a few words spoken, followed by a few drops of water sprinkled, by an unknown man in a faraway town didn't seem a lot to ask in return for lifesaving medical care.

By this time Raymond had been placed in a specially equipped incubator to allow him to travel in an ambulance. A number of doctors, nurses and ambulance personnel were busying themselves around it, out in the hospital corridor, making vital and final preparations for the journey.

As they began to wheel the incubator towards the exit, Esther followed it, broken-hearted and bewildered. She was dressed to go home and had been quite happy to accept that Raymond would be staying behind in hospital for a few days. What she couldn't come to terms with, however, was that he was now critically ill and was being whisked away out of her world and care completely, into some distant realm of anguish and uncertainty.

What was really the matter with him, that was causing the medical staff such obvious concern, she wondered.

Where was he going?

Would they be good to him?

What could they do for them in Drogheda that couldn't be done in Monaghan?

And most important of all, could his tiny, fragile frame survive all this?

It was all so hard to take in, for it was all happening so suddenly.

When the anxious cluster was passing the ward she had just left Esther called in to Frances who was waiting for her sister to return so that she could accompany her home, "Bring my bag!"

Just before they arrived at the lift to go down to the ground floor Trevor came dashing up the stairs. As he turned left to go along the corridor he met the frenzied procession coming in the opposite direction. The first thing to catch his eye was the incubator being rushed along by an ambulance man. He was followed, and surrounded, by the doctors, nurses and the other member of his crew.

In the middle of all this flurry of activity was Esther.

His grief-stricken wife was weeping uncontrollably.

Trevor pushed in beside her and joined the group whose sole aim was to rush that incubator out to the ambulance, which had been left reversed right up to the main door of the hospital, with its back doors open and its engines running, in the shortest possible time.

The two ambulance men and a nurse secured the incubator in the ambulance, and when they closed the back door they began their journey straight away.

The door was no sooner closed than Trevor, who had been standing with his arm around his now shivering and shaking as well as weeping, wife, cried, "Come on you two. We are going too."

With that Trevor, Esther and Frances made their way, as quickly as Esther's condition would allow, over to Trevor's car, which was parked just across from the ambulance.

As it set off at speed down the hospital drive, with its blue light flashing, Trevor, his wife and sister-in-law were right behind it.

"What are we going to do, Trevor?" Esther asked frantically.

"Follow it as far as we can," came the immediate reply. "You are not fit to go all the way to Drogheda, but we will go a bit!"

They hadn't been given much time to formulate any organised strategy. Events had overtaken them at a startling pace and they were at their wits' end. It had become a case of thinking their way through the crisis as it unfolded around them.

"And there is Darren as well," Esther went on. She was back on the verge of hysterics. "I need to see him, and we will have to make arrangements for somebody to look after him before we go anywhere!"

This conversation took place as Trevor was tailing a speeding ambulance through the mid-afternoon traffic in Monaghan town.

Having left the centre of town the ambulance began to go even faster as it set off out the Dublin Road and up Cathedral Hill.

It was there, too, that Trevor, the driver of the hurtling blue Hillman Avenger, was faced with a snap decision. He was coming to a fork in the road.

As they approached the cathedral, he took the only sensible, but nonetheless difficult, course of action.

The ambulance veered off to the right.

It was on its way to Drogheda, with their little son.

Trevor and Esther veered off to the left.

They were on their way home. Without him.

6

BETTER THE DOG THAN THE CHILD

Next morning Frances arrived up into the bedroom to Esther. She stood nervously at the side of the bed. Esther sensed her unease.

Trevor had left much earlier for his work in the bakery and Darren was asleep.

Frances had been putting off this moment but recognised that she could delay it no longer. How, though, was her sister, who had been through so much in the previous few days, going to come to terms with yet more bad news?

"Esther, I don't know how to break this to you, on top of everything else," she began, "but your dog has died. I found him dead when I went outside this morning."

Esther began to cry again. She had cried more the day before than she had ever done in one single day in her life up until that point, and now she was at it again. Shan had been a good dog and Trevor and she had been very fond of him. They would miss him about the place, coming to meet them with a friendly bark.

In a few minutes, however, she stopped crying almost as suddenly and spontaneously as she had started. It seemed as though she had discovered a secret formula for the instant drying of tears.

A thought struck her like a bolt from the blue. Better the dog than the child, it said. As she contemplated this sentiment before voicing it to her sister, Esther felt a strange sense of peace enfold her. She was convinced that although the dog had died Raymond was going to live, despite having to be rushed away to another hospital, critically ill.

All that mattered to her at that moment was seeing him again. She had barely slept the night before wondering about him. It had been great to be home with little Darren once more, and he could scarcely conceal his delight at seeing his mum again, but what, she kept asking herself, had become of baby Raymond?

It was later that day before she found out, before her question was answered.

Trevor had asked off early from work and he and Esther, who was still desperately weak, set off to drive the fifty-four miles to Drogheda in the late afternoon. It was almost seven o'clock in the evening before they arrived outside the hospital.

Having entered the building they followed the arrows to the children's ward and were then escorted by a member of the nursing staff though a set of doors leading into the baby unit. The anxious parents were met there by a trainee nurse who asked them to wait until she contacted a senior member of staff who would take them to Raymond.

As they stood by the nursing station, awaiting the return of someone qualified to take them on the short but final leg of their trip to find their little son, their attention was attracted to a baby behind a huge glass panel in a small ward opposite.

Trevor and Esther stood motionless and mesmerised. They couldn't take their eyes off the scene behind the glass.

A baby was lying in a cot that was covered by a canopy from which hung two ultra-violet lights. The infant was lying on its back and was wearing only a nappy. Its arms were spread out wide on either side and its hands were bandaged and tied to the cot rails. There was a needle in its temple and its eyes were swathed in bandages. A tube protruded from its nose and a collection of wires radiated in different directions from pads affixed to its chest. The baby also had a drip in its heel.

The blue lights added an eerie touch to the scene, for they made the baby's skin appear deathly pale, almost transparent.

It was a shocking sight to the inexperienced eye. Trevor found it scary, like something out of a horror movie. To Esther it was simply the most pathetic scene she had ever witnessed.

"If that's my baby I'll go mad!" she said, airing her pent-up feelings to her husband who was struggling desperately to satisfy himself that it *wasn't* their baby.

"No, Esther. There's no way. That just couldn't be our wee Raymond," he replied, in a valiant but vain attempt to console her.

The longer they stood and the more intently they looked, the more Trevor and Esther were convinced, without expressing it to each other, that the baby in the blue-light cot was their little baby son. Despite the array of tubes and wires, pads and bandages, that had almost camouflaged his identity, both parents, who had each held their son on separate occasions, were beset with a growing suspicion that this was indeed him.

And their premonition proved correct.

When the senior nurse appeared she greeted them with a cheery, "Nice to meet you, Mr. and Mrs. Gillanders, Raymond is over here." With that she set off a step ahead of them to the ward across the way.

She understood how the anxious parents must be feeling, having dealt with concerned couples like Trevor and Esther many times before. Not only did she appreciate how perturbed such parents must feel at seeing their little loved one in that upsetting condition and position, however, but she had also become expert in allaying all their understandable fears.

Before Raymond's mum and dad could even make a comment or ask a question she launched into an explanation of the medical equipment surrounding the cot and the state of their son in it.

"Don't get annoyed at all the wires and tubes around him," she said. "They are all there for a particular reason. Each one is designed to help him in some way." She then proceeded to explain the purpose of each of them.

Having finished that, she went on to say, "Don't be panicking either because his eyes and hands are bandaged. His hands are bandaged and tied to prevent him from pulling out his tubes and drips. The bandages on his eyes are to protect them from the ultraviolet light."

The nurse then switched off the light so that all three of them could approach the cot. Esther's first reaction was to want to lift him out but the nurse told her that it would be a few days before they were satisfied that his condition had stabilised sufficiently to allow him to be handled.

It was almost a week before all the tubes and wires had been removed and Esther had the joy of taking little Raymond on her knee. Over the next few visits the staff taught her how to prepare, and then give him a tube feed, but they also encouraged her to try and train him with a bottle, to teach him how to suck. This was a slow process, as the baby's energy level was so low, but Esther didn't mind. She was quite happy to nurse him for two hours and have him take at most ten millilitres of milk. It was a labour of love.

Raymond had been almost three weeks in hospital and seemed to be making some progress when Professor Ann Murphy, the consultant paediatrician in the children's unit, joined Trevor and Esther in the little ward where they were sitting feeding him one afternoon. The young parents had been impressed by the manner in which they had been kept well informed of all the different aspects of Raymond's condition by Professor Murphy and her staff.

That afternoon she was, she said, in a position to give them the results of the tests that had been conducted some weeks before. These had been designed to examine the extent of the problem with Raymond's heart.

The tests had revealed that he had congenital heart disease and that his heart and liver were both enlarged. Professor Murphy went on to explain that with this combination of conditions it was highly unlikely that they would ever be able to operate on his heart.

The prognosis was not good, but Trevor and Esther, who had by then become so engrossed in little Raymond's progress either didn't recognise, or chose subconsciously not to recognise, how ill he really was.

All they could talk about was how well he was improving at taking his bottle.

Finally, after Raymond had spent the first six weeks of his life in hospital, and his parents had spent those same six weeks driving a more than one hundred mile round trip to go and visit him, the big day came.

Raymond had begun to take sufficient from his daily bottle feeds to nourish him, and the hospital staff considered him well enough to be allowed to go home.

How would his young parents cope with a chronically ill Down's syndrome son?

How would two year-old Darren react to having a baby brother, who was obviously going to demand a lot of his parent's, and particularly his mum's, attention, in the house?

Whatever happened, it would be important that Raymond's parents and brother showed him all the love and care they could muster.

7

OUR WEE MONTY

Trevor and Esther had been planning for Raymond's discharge from hospital for weeks. They had always believed that the day would come when their little one would be fully integrated into the family at home in Monaghan. And when the day came they were ready.

As part of the preparations they had a cot especially designed in order to keep him in the living room with them all the time. It was smaller than the standard baby cot and open all the way round so that Raymond could always see out of it and his loving parents and big brother could always see in. Trevor and Esther were determined that Raymond would be given all the attention he needed both day and night. They provided not only endless loving care but also a range of mental stimulation by surrounding his cot with a variety of educational toys and mobiles.

Whatever reservations they had in the backs of their minds about how Darren would accept this new addition to the household, and if he would feel sidelined by his arrival, proved totally groundless.

He adopted a most loving and protective attitude to his little brother from the hour he first entered the house. The bonding between them was instantaneous

Darren became Raymond's constant companion. Big brother would play beside his cot for hours, allowing Raymond, who appeared to dote on him, to follow his every movement, wherever he went, whatever he did. Mum and dad's warm-hearted approach to Raymond had been automatically and subconsciously transmitted to Darren who displayed a maturity well beyond his tender years when dealing with his little brother.

Trevor and Esther were often amazed at his patience. One of the games, which afforded Raymond endless enjoyment, as he grew older, was pulling off his socks and throwing them away. It was a simple, harmless activity, but since it was vital that he did not become too cold Darren would put them on again, only for the process to be repeated many times. Raymond had only been home a few months when Darren was able to remind his mum that it was 'time for wee Monty's medicine.'

This was his pet name. None of the family knew where it came from, or who had first used it, but Trevor, Esther and Darren all began to refer to him as 'our wee Monty.'

Raymond's heart, and hence his general physical condition, were so weak, that it was important that he was not allowed to cry for long periods. This didn't ever happen, for two reasons.

Firstly Raymond was by nature a happy, placid child, not much disposed to cry. On the very rare occasions when he did attempt it, however, there was always someone at hand, either, mum, dad, big brother or some of the regular visitors who had fallen under the spell of 'wee Monty,' to comfort him and attend to his needs.

His immediate family and the wider family circle all loved him but he also built up an adoring fan club who called regularly just to be in his company. He had a habit of melting the hearts of all who came in contact with him.

There were three girls from the town, all in their late teens, who called at different times to spend an afternoon caring for Raymond. Mary, Jane and Jenny appeared to be quite in their element sitting beside his cot and entertaining him.

Esther was often amazed at the devotion of these girls to Raymond. She was particularly impressed one day when she had taken Mary with her into town on a shopping trip. As she carried her precious charge from one shop to another in her arms, so that he could see all around him, Mary was obviously 'as proud as a peacock.' When Esther and she stopped occasionally to speak to people they knew in the supermarket 'Monty' charmed them with a winning smile.

This often caused his mum to reflect on, and feel slightly guilty about, the painful days leading up to, and immediately following his birth. Why, she wondered, did I ever worry about having this little boy when he is capable of giving so much pleasure to so many people?

Violet had continued to keep contact with Trevor and Esther during Raymond's prolonged stay in hospital and after he came home she supported the family in any way she could. She was a member of the Cavan and Monaghan Down's Syndrome Association and encouraged Trevor and Esther to join, assuring them that they would find it helpful.

And it turned out to be even more useful than they had expected. Although Raymond was the only child who had a heart condition as well as being Down's syndrome in the Association, his parents found it reassuring to realise that there were other 'Down's' children across the two counties who were obviously very happy, and making progress.

Another benefit of membership of the Association was that during the monthly meetings the parents gained useful information on various aspects of working with their children. Esther was soon to learn that one of the most valuable ways to help her little son, and to enjoy the charisma of his company as she did so was to massage his skin daily with lanolin cream.

'Wee Monty' looked forward to these daily sessions so much, becoming very excited when his mum appeared with the huge jar of lanolin cream. He smiled contentedly when she began to massage him gently from head to toe.

Trevor, Esther and big brother Darren regarded every day they had Raymond at home as a bonus. He still had serious problems with heart failure and occasional bouts of pneumonia and these meant that his parents had to make frequent trips to the hospital in Drogheda with him for treatment. There wasn't a month out of the first year from he was discharged from hospital that Raymond didn't have to be rushed to Drogheda at least once.

When Raymond was almost a year old, in the summer of 1982, the hospital in Drogheda arranged an appointment for his parents with a consultant in Dublin. He, they said, would be able to assess Raymond's condition and tell them whether he would be able to perform heart surgery at a later date to help increase his life expectancy.

When the consultant had examined him, and studied the medical data from the hospital in Drogheda, he gave them his diagnosis.

Raymond's heart was so enlarged that it would be impossible to operate on it and he estimated that he would live until he was six years of age at the most.

To the surprise of some, Trevor and Esther were more delighted than disturbed to be given this news. They were well aware that their 'Wee Monty' was a very sick child, and if he could be spared to bring his unique contribution of love and joy into their lives for another five years it would be wonderful!

8

LETTER FROM AMERICA

The letter from America came as a complete surprise one morning. Trevor and Esther weren't normally sent much through the post except bills, so to receive a letter with an American stamp was most unusual.

When Esther opened it she was pleased and puzzled all at once. She considered it amazing that someone from a faraway country would ever be interested enough to take the time to write to them in Monaghan. As she read through it, though, her astonishment did not abate but she began to understand, at least in part, the loving, caring motive that had inspired it.

The lady who had sent it explained that Esther's cousin Lenny, who was a friend of hers, had told her about little Raymond and his condition. She went on to say that she and her husband had a son, Chad, who was Down's syndrome and was growing up to enjoy a happy and fulfilled life in many ways.

It was touching to receive the letter, and encouraging to learn of

Chad's development, but it was the quotation and the promise at the end of it that left Esther somewhat bemused. The words that the writer quoted in the course of her letter were, she said, from the Bible. Esther had never seen or heard them before and found them rather strange.

'And we know that all things work together for good to them that love God,' they declared. The kind lady who had written to Trevor and Esther said that she was Christian and had learnt to accept that whatever happened to her in life was part of God's plan for her. This was a totally new concept to the couple in Monaghan and Esther in particular struggled with it.

How, she wondered, as she looked at her precious little Raymond, with his incurable heart complaint that required frequent visits to a specialist hospital more than fifty miles away, could his condition be 'working together for good,' for anybody?

The promise at the end of the letter was a new one on her, too. The writer had finished it off by assuring Trevor and Esther that she and her husband would 'be praying for them, and the two boys.' That was very kind of them, Esther mused, deeply appreciating their thoughtfulness and sincerity, but what were they going to pray for?

Esther wrote back, thanking the lady for her letter, and within a month she had a reply. This time it was a personal letter, as mother to mother, but the writer had also gone to the trouble to enclose a small book, which she hoped Esther would find 'helpful.'

It was Dale Evans Rogers' book 'Angel Unaware,' the story of her little Down's syndrome daughter, Robin. The book was written from an imaginative perspective, with Robin, who had died, recounting her story from heaven, Up Here, as she calls it. Esther was able to identify with so many of the situations and conditions described by the imaginary 'Angel Unaware,' however, that she found it gripping. The incidents reported to have taken place Down There (on earth) rang so true for her, and portrayed Raymond's position so accurately and sensitively that she found herself returning to read the book over and over again.

As she did so Esther gradually became increasingly aware of a sense that neither she, nor Trevor, nor Raymond, nor Darren, nor for that matter anybody at all was here forever. They had been told that

Raymond would be with them for six years at the most.

His dad and she had been delighted to hear that. But if he were to be spared to them for six years, and then die, what would happen to him? What then?

She shared her feelings with Trevor, only to realise that he, too, had become gripped with an awareness of a life after death. The young couple began to discuss these matters together. They realised, in a strange way, as though prompted by a supernatural perception, that if Raymond were to die he would go straight to heaven. That same sense also caused them to recognise that if they were to be in heaven with him there would have to be some kind of a change in their lives. They knew that they would have to 'make their peace with God' before they could ever join him there, but had no idea where, or how, that peace could be found.

This growing consciousness of God and a life after death led Trevor and Esther into thinking often about Raymond and his future. Perhaps coloured by the imagery of 'Angel Unawares', they each began to dream separately of his funeral and his reception into heaven. When they shared what they could remember of these dreams with one another they were often struck by the similarities between them.

The relatively transient nature of time, the inevitability of death, a developing appreciation of a powerful and eternal God and an acknowledgement of an after-earth existence was beginning to surround them.

Although this creeping awareness had begun to invade the background of their lives, Trevor and Esther continued to be very much involved in enjoying every possible moment with Raymond and attending to his many physical needs.

Whilst his serious heart problems had always remained their predominant concern, the thrush, which had broken out in his mouth, was also a worry. Raymond had to take so many different medicines for his various complaints that they had triggered an unpleasant reaction.

Proprietary cures seemed to have no effect on this condition, so when Esther heard one day of 'a man who had a charm for thrush' she told Trevor about it when he arrived home from work. This man was reputed to be 'the seventh son of the seventh son,' and in Irish folklore such people were supposedly endowed with unusual abilities.

Trevor agreed with his wife that 'anything was worth a try,' and after having made a few more enquiries they took Raymond out to the man's home one evening. When there the 'man with the charm' uttered a few words, bent over Raymond and then blew three times into his mouth. This would not be considered as recommended medical practice by some, but it worked. Raymond's mouth, which was heavily infected, had completely cleared up by the following morning.

The concerned parents were astounded, and extremely pleased. Soon their minds were off on another tack. If a man with a charm can cure thrush, they began to think, is there not somebody out there with a charm for heart complaints?

Apparently there was.

When some of their acquaintances heard of the healing of the thrush, they were quick to tell Trevor and Esther of a friend of a friend of theirs who knew a man, 'away out in the country, who had a charm for bad hearts.'

That was the very man Trevor and Esther had been looking for and they lost little time in driving their apparently incurable second son 'away out into the country,' to see him. Perhaps his charm would be more powerful than medical science.

Their high hopes were soon to be dashed, however, for it soon became clear that it hadn't worked.

Raymond's condition didn't improve. He had to be rushed to Drogheda for treatment a few days after he had been taken to the man with the charm.

What were Trevor and Esther to do now?

They had become desperate to source a cure for Raymond's heart condition. As their little son grew older, and more endearing by the day, the prospect of ever having to part with him became even more painful.

So where next?

9

COULD YOU FOLLOW?

A visit to 'the man of God' would at least be a start.

The worried parents had heard Trevor's aunt Edna speak often of a preacher called Sam Workman who was what she described as 'a real man of God with a great ministry of prayer and healing.' When she contacted them with the news that Rev. Workman was coming to conduct meetings in the Hillgrove Hotel in Monaghan they determined to pay him a call at some stage. They thought that if they were to ask him to pray for Raymond perhaps he could be healed from his distressing heart condition. Anything, they reckoned, was worth a try.

One evening, during the first week of the meetings in Monaghan, Trevor and Esther resolved to seek an audience with the speaker. They arranged for someone to stay with Darren and Raymond and as they drove down to the hotel they discussed their plan of action. It would seem pointless for both of them to go in at first, they concluded, and so decided that Trevor would go into the hotel, locate 'the man of God,' and ask him to pray for Raymond. If, at that stage, Esther's presence was required, then Trevor could come out for her.

One of the first people Trevor encountered in the foyer of the Hillgrove was his uncle Andy, who was there to direct those wishing to attend the meeting in half an hour's time to the correct room. Uncle Andy stepped forward and greeted his nephew warmly. He was pleased, but not entirely surprised to see him, for Edna, his wife, had forewarned him to 'look out for Trevor and Esther,' for they were 'thinking of going down to speak to Rev. Workman some night.'

"Would there be any chance of me seeing Mr Workman, or is he not here yet?" Trevor enquired of his uncle. "Esther and I were wondering if we could ask him to pray for Raymond."

"He's here O.K.," Uncle Andy replied, "but he is already in the prayer meeting. That's no problem, though. If you just stay there a minute I'll bring him out to meet you." With that he set off to fetch the speaker and Trevor was left to his thoughts.

'The prayer meeting,' sounded hopeful, but just a little scary. Since he was unaware up until that time of the custom of evangelical Christians to hold prayer meetings before most services, Trevor wondered what they could be praying about. Somebody else's child, perhaps? And would he have to go into 'the prayer meeting,' and tell whoever was in there all about Raymond? Would Esther have to come in too…?

His musings were interrupted when Uncle Andy returned a few minutes later with another gentleman, whom he assumed to be Mr. Workman.

The preacher reached out a hand to shake hands with Trevor and then introduced himself in such a warm and friendly way that the young father felt immediately at ease.

"I'm Sammy Workman," he began. "Great to meet you, Trevor. Let's find a quiet spot somewhere to have a chat."

With that Uncle Andy directed them to a small room where they could remain undisturbed for as long as they wished. Trevor appreciated the fact that Mr. Workman had taken time out from his prayer meeting and so lost no time in telling him about Raymond. The well-known speaker sat and listened with obvious interest as Trevor recounted the story of his little son's birth, the discovery and complexity of his heart condition, and the fact that under normal circumstances he would only have at most six years to live.

When he had finished Rev. Workman said, "Thanks, Trevor for sharing all that with me. I can see that you and your wife love little Raymond very much. Let us commend him, and you, to the Lord in prayer."

The 'man of God' then bowed his head and began to pray. Trevor was immediately impressed. He had never heard anybody addressing God like this before. He spoke reverently and respectfully but it was still as though he were in intimate contact with Him. It was as if he expected a response to his requests because they were presented in the 'Name of the Lord Jesus.'

As Trevor sat listening he was moved, not only by the personal nature of the prayer, but also by its content. It soon became clear that Mr. Workman had been paying particular attention to what Trevor had been telling him, for he mentioned specific aspects of Raymond's condition in his prayer, as he besought God earnestly to heal the ailing child, if it were His will. Having presented Raymond's needs before God in some detail Rev. Workman then went on to pray for his parents. Trevor was surprised and touched by this. He recognised that in Sam Workman he had encountered someone who was genuinely concerned for people, and longed that they may come into the vital relationship with God that he enjoyed,

As Mr. Workman prayed that Trevor and Esther would come to know the Lord in a personal way, and experience His peace and guidance in their lives, Trevor was amazed. It was all so gracious, and yet so real and patently of utmost importance to the praying minister that he considered himself strangely privileged and enriched to have heard him pray, not only for his baby son, but also for himself. The prayer had comforted him, but also made him aware that it was possible to have a relationship with God that he knew nothing about.

Minutes later, having thanked Rev. Workman profusely for praying with such concern for Raymond, Trevor was out in the car telling Esther about Rev. Workman's gracious attitude, and his remarkable prayer, not only for Raymond, but also for them.

How, they wondered, could they thank him for taking the time to pray for Raymond? It was clear that he did not require any financial reward for his services so Trevor and Esther decided that since they had the remainder of the evening free the least they could do was to go to his meeting. Doing that, they reasoned, would be one way in which to register their appreciation for his intercession for their son.

They sat out in the car until a quarter to eight when a number of people arrived beside them in the car park and began making their way into the hotel, singly, in pairs, or in small mumbling groups, presumably to Rev. Workman's meeting.

When Trevor and Esther considered that there was a strong enough stream of people flowing into the hotel for them to make an unobtrusive entrance they went in too. Their attempts to remain inconspicuous proved unsuccessful, however, for Trevor and Esther were well known in the town, and when the stewards saw them come in they welcomed them with genuine warmth and enthusiasm. The unquestionable sincerity with which they greeted the young couple, who were making their first appearance at the mission out of a sense of obligation to the preacher rather than any real desire to hear his message, made them feel special.

Having been shown to a seat on the right-hand side of the large function room in the hotel Trevor and Esther had ten minutes to acclimatise to their new surroundings before the service began. As they looked around they found that the room was filling up fast and there was a buzz of expectation about the place. Someone was playing hymn tunes on the piano and people were talking to one another with a muted anticipation. It struck Esther that some of these people had probably been counting the hours all day, not able to wait to get there. Clearly this was going to prove different from any church service they had ever attended before!

The newcomers found the wholehearted nature of the singing and the earnestness of the opening prayer heart-warming, though unfamiliar, but it was the conviction with which Mr. Workman delivered his message that impressed them most.

Nobody could be in any doubt that this man believed

passionately every word he preached. He was in earnest. What he had to say was important to him, and he saw it as his role in life to convince his audience that it was of prime importance to them as well.

He read from John chapter ten in the Bible and told his congregation that he was going to speak to them that evening about the Good Shepherd. He explained that The Good Shepherd in the story was in fact Jesus, the One who had 'given His life for the sheep.'

Although this sermon was delivered with great sincerity neither Trevor nor Esther found it especially striking. They were only there, after all, out of a sense of duty, not a desire to learn about either God or themselves, or any particular or pressing wish to change the pattern of their lives.

There was one illustration, however, which Rev. Workman used towards the close of his address, that transported Esther from her state of indifference to the realm of reality, all in an instant.

He told of the practice often used by shepherds to entice reluctant ewes into the sheepfold. "They will often lift a little lamb and carry it into the sheepfold, and the mother will invariably follow, attracted by the cries of her offspring," he said.

Then, by way of applying his illustration to his message for the evening he asked the pointed question, "If God were to take your little lamb into his heavenly sheepfold could you follow?"

Esther was pierced to the heart.

If God were to take her little lamb to Himself she couldn't follow. She knew she wasn't ready.

10

WHAT'S THE RUSH?

The baby-sitter had arrived. Everything was arranged.

It was late November 1982 and Trevor and Esther had bought tickets for a dance in Monaghan. This was a fund-raising event, organised by the local Down's Syndrome Association, in which they had become increasingly involved. It was to be their first big night out together since Raymond was born, but Esther had mixed feelings about it. She tried to tell herself that it would 'be great to have a night out together,' but deep down she had her reservations.

They were to travel to the dance with Trevor's sister Jacqueline, and George, her boyfriend, but they were late in arriving at the house to pick up the young parents. As they walked around the house, all dressed up, but still going nowhere, Esther said to her husband, "I don't think wee Monty's very well tonight."

"Don't worry, Esther. He will be all right. You are just fretting because you don't really want to leave him," Trevor told her.

The baby-sitter took up the same theme.

"Don't worry, Esther," she said, repeating Trevor's advice. "He will be fine. Go on to the dance and enjoy yourselves."

Esther was not convinced.

Ten minutes later, and with George and Jackie still not arrived, she took Raymond's temperature and found that it was very high.

"I don't think we should go to the dance tonight," she told Trevor. "I think we would be better to take Raymond down to the doctor's straight away."

Recognising that an anxious wife and mother could never be a totally carefree dance partner, and that there actually *was* something the matter with 'wee Monty, despite his attempts to persuade Esther to the contrary, Trevor agreed to take them both down to the surgery. When the doctor examined little Raymond her instruction was brief and to the point. "I would advise you to take him to Drogheda straight away. He is in heart failure," she said.

That meant a total change of plan for the evening. The baby-sitter looked after Darren while Trevor and Esther set out, not for a dance, but for a hospital in Drogheda.

As soon as they arrived there, the staff, who had become familiar with Raymond and his condition put him in an oxygen tent and on a drip and within a few days he was stabilised and out of danger yet again.

The doctors kept Raymond in hospital for two weeks before satisfying themselves that he was well enough to be discharged, but when he came home Trevor and Esther were conscious of a deterioration in his condition. It was obvious that his energy levels had dropped. He was once able to roll around the floor, following every noise and often arriving at his mum's feet in the kitchen, having rolled from where she had left him on the living room floor. Now he just sat still on his mat for long periods. This was unusual. It seemed that the spark of life that often gave him an appealing but mischievous look, had been extinguished.

Trevor and Esther and family had been invited to spend Christmas with Frances and her husband and during those days Esther's sister gained some insight into what it meant to care for a very sick child. The parents were up often during the night with Raymond whose breathing had become noisy and very rapid when he was in his cot.

The abnormal sound of his breathing and the constant attention Trevor and Esther lavished so unstintingly on their 'wee Monty,' caused Francis to remark once, in a mixture of awe and admiration, "I don't know how you pair listen to that laboured breathing day in day out. It would do my head in."

Back home after Christmas Raymond still showed little interest in his surroundings, and this was strange. His parents were concerned about this but always kept hoping that one day he would improve and they would catch that impish glint in his eye once again. What would they not give to see him rolling round the floor at their feet as he used to do?

It didn't happen, but instead, on Wednesday, January 12, 1983, his condition took a dramatic turn for the worse.

Trevor had left for work early in the morning and when Esther went up to lift Raymond from his cot to wash and dress him for the day there was blood on his face.

"Has that wee nose of yours been bleeding again?" she said as she lifted him out. It was a futile exercise in self-deception. Esther was trying valiantly to make herself believe that the blood on her 'wee Monty's' face was the result of a nose-bleed during the night.

Her maternal instincts, that had never proved wrong to date, told her that it wasn't, however. It was something much more sinister than that.

When she brought him downstairs Esther dressed him and watched him carefully. It would be important to catch any further hint of bleeding as soon as it occurred.

Although Raymond seemed uncharacteristically restless, and he whimpered softly to himself once or twice, nothing further happened for an hour or so.

Esther was beginning to half-believe that maybe the blood on his face was a mere isolated incident until she was working at the sink in the kitchen. Unwilling to leave Raymond on his rug in the living room as she normally would have done in his more settled spells, she had placed him in his push-chair and brought him in beside her.

When half-way through washing the dishes she turned to look down and say something to her little son, who was nestled in close to her side.

She stopped in shock with her hands held dripping just a few inches above the suds on the surface of the water. Blood was spurting out of Raymond's mouth in short, gurgling bursts.

This was the development that Esther had dreaded. It was the spur to immediate action. Raymond was in heart failure once more.

Having changed his clothes Esther set off with Raymond in the push-chair. Not having a telephone meant that the fastest way to procure the services of a doctor was to hot-foot it to the surgery.

She hurtled down the road as fast as she could, but her first stop was not the doctor's surgery. It was nearly noon and that was the time Darren had to be collected from Nursery School. Although she arrived almost ten minutes before bell-time it didn't even cross Esther's mind to go in and ask to have Darren out a few minutes early. That kind of thing just wasn't done.

As she waited impatiently with the other mothers outside the Nursery one of them said, "Look, Esther, your wee boy is bringing up blood."

"I know," Esther replied. "I am on my way down to the doctor's, but I had to stop off and collect Darren, for I hadn't time to tell anybody else to call for him."

When she arrived at the surgery Esther was given priority to take Raymond in to see the doctor and her instruction was the same as it had been on the night of the dance back in November, "Take him up to the hospital in Drogheda straight away."

That meant another walk across the town to the bakery where Trevor worked to see if he could be released early to drive his terribly sick son the fifty-four miles to Drogheda. Never once in the duration of Raymond's illness were his parents offered the facility of an ambulance other than on the first night when his incubator was taken to hospital in one.

It took fifteen minutes to reach the bakery with a desperately ill baby in the push-chair and three year-old Darren striding manfully along, as fast as his legs could carry him, beside it. When the trio arrived at Trevor's place of work he only had to take one look at Raymond to know that something was terribly wrong. Esther told him the story in short gasps, and he asked his boss for time off, explaining that Raymond had to be taken to hospital immediately.

Trevor was released without question and within minutes he had bundled Esther and the children into the car and they were on their way home to prepare for yet another dramatic dash to Drogheda.

During their brief stop in the house Esther placed Raymond on his favourite spot on the mat in front of the fire while Trevor and she made final preparations for the journey. He would be safe enough now for there would always be someone around to watch him.

Trevor was moving hurriedly around the house, changing out of his baker's outfit and leaving a trail of flour dust in his wake. In his haste it seemed that he couldn't find the clothes, and then the shoes, that he wanted to change into.

On one of his excursions through the living room he glanced across at 'wee Monty.' His little son was deathly pale. His fair skin appeared almost transparent. Their eyes met.

It was enough to stop Trevor in his step. There seemed to be a message in baby Raymond's peculiarly puzzled expression. It looked as though he were trying to say, "What are you rushing around like that for? What is life all about?"

The thought struck Trevor like a hammer-blow.

Surely there must be something deeper, something more lasting, and certainly something more satisfying to life than I have yet discovered, he mused.

And if there is, where, or how, do I find it?

11

I'M NOT STOPPING FOR ANYBODY!

In less than fifteen minutes the turn-around was complete.

Trevor had changed his clothes, a baby-sitter had arrived to collect Darren and take him to her home, and Esther had wrapped little Raymond up warmly for the drive to Drogheda. And what a drive it was!

They left their home in Monaghan shortly after one o'clock and sped off down the road. Trevor switched on the hazard lights as he raced along. This was probably in the hope that the sense of extreme urgency and utter desperation, which had possessed him, would somehow be mirrored on the outside of the speeding vehicle. Could it possibly exonerate him from having to observe the speed limits in the towns and villages that flashed past in a blur of houses, shops and unrecognisable people?

Once, along the road, they zoomed past a man who tried to flag them down. "Oh Trevor, look, that man has had a puncture. Should we not stop to help him?" Esther exclaimed, instinctively. Although she had a gravely ill child on her knee her instant reaction to someone else in need was to try and afford what assistance she could.

"It may sound cruel to you Esther, " her husband replied, visibly tightening his grip on the steering wheel. "But we will let somebody else in less of a hurry than us help him. I'm not stopping for anybody!"

He considered his apparent lack of compassion for a stranded fellow-motorist justified as he kept glancing anxiously across at Raymond on Esther's knee. His little son was still deathly pale. There were times when his body appeared to go limp and floppy, like a rag doll. His shallow breathing came in laboured gasps.

Esther held him lovingly. She thought, more than once, that life was ebbing out of the tiny, drooping body. "If only we can get him to an oxygen tent in time," she kept saying, occasionally audibly to Trevor, but mostly inwardly to herself. Having articulated this goal many times she then began to turn it into a desperate prayer. "Oh God, please help us to get Raymond to the hospital and into an oxygen tent before anything happens to him," she breathed with panic-stricken urgency.

They were relieved to reach the hospital with their precious 'wee Monty' still breathing, but were taken aback when the doctor came to make his diagnosis.

As he was examining Raymond he noticed a series of tiny red dots, like pin pricks, on his skin. "I'm not happy with these little red spots," he told the already distraught parents. "They are a sign of meningitis. We are gong to have to do a lumbar puncture to rule that out."

Trevor and Esther were most annoyed. "He hasn't got meningitis," they objected. "He has had those little dots on his skin before. He is in heart failure. We know for we have seen him like this many times."

The doctor wasn't listening. He was the professional and as far as he was concerned Raymond was going to have a lumbar puncture. Choosing to ignore the parents' protests he instructed a nurse to take him to another room down the corridor where this procedure was to be carried out.

Raymond's parents were not permitted to be present when the lumbar puncture was being done and so were obliged to wait out in the corridor. Their previous annoyance turned to outright anger as they heard their little son scream wildly during what they considered to be an unnecessary exercise.

"This should never have happened to a sick child with a chronic heart condition," Trevor fumed. Esther, who was equally enraged, interspersed her outbursts of anger with periods of uncontrollable crying. "This is enough to kill him," she blurted and blustered through her tears. "He was nearly gone a couple of times on the way up, so how will he ever survive the like of this?"

When Raymond's screams subsided Trevor and Esther assumed that the most painful part of the ordeal was over and were left to wonder how it would have affected their little one. They didn't have long to wait, however, for the door soon opened and a nurse emerged carrying Raymond. He was obviously distressed, but at least his mum and dad's imagined worst-case scenario had not taken place. He had survived.

The nurse brought Raymond back to the children's ward where he was placed in an oxygen tent in a 'high observation' position near the nurses' station. "If they had only done that in the first place," Esther remarked to Trevor when they witnessed the calming effect it seemed to have on him. Within an hour he had settled sufficiently to be drifting off to sleep. It was as though he appeared relieved to be in the oxygen tent. He seemed to feel relaxed and secure in it after all the trauma of the previous few hours.

Trevor and Esther sat watching him, and as they did so the tensions that had tortured them since leaving Monaghan gradually melted away. Their 'little Monty' was now in the best possible place for him.

They were even further reassured when Raymond, who had been lying facing the window into the nurses' room turned himself right around to look at his mum and dad. When he realised that they were beside him he reached up and placed his hand against the plastic of the tent. This was something that he and his parents had developed during Raymond's frequent visits to oxygen tents. When he put his hand up against the plastic it was a sign that he wanted either of them to place their hand over his.

Tears welled up in Esther's already reddened eyes when she saw him do this and she immediately put her hand against his. This was all the contact the confines of an oxygen tent would allow, but it was enough. They were all in touch again. Raymond was obviously comforted by the contact too for he soon slipped into a sounder sleep.

With their sick son now settled to some degree, Trevor and Esther sat discussing what to do next. As afternoon wore on into evening and other parents came and went in the children's ward, Esther raised an issue which she had never before contemplated during the course of all Raymond's previous visits to hospital. Should she plan to stay the night with him?

They considered all the options. It was clear that Trevor would be expected in at work in the bakery early next morning so he would definitely have to go home. What about Esther, though? What should she do?

Having thought it through carefully, she decided, despite the desperate tug of her motherly instincts, to go home with her husband. When she took into account that she didn't have enough money to buy herself food until Trevor would return the next evening, she didn't have a change of clothes, nor had she made any arrangements to have Darren cared for, it seemed that she would have to go. This decision was reinforced by the fact that although her natural, maternal desire was to be with her ailing child, the hospital hadn't encouraged her to consider it necessary.

It was after midnight when Trevor and she eventually left the ward to start on their journey back home. They found it extremely difficult to leave little Raymond after all that he had been through, but at least he was sleeping peacefully when they whispered goodbye to him outside his oxygen tent.

It was a clear, cold winter's night as Trevor and Esther drove home. There was very little traffic on the roads so they made good progress. Neither parent had much to say in the car as they were both lost in thought, looking back on the hectic events of the day. At one stage Trevor, who had come to reflecting on the breakneck journey to the hospital, broke the silence to remark, "I just wish the roads had been as clear as this when we were coming up."

They were nearing home when the car spluttered to a stop. Trevor, who had vowed on the drive to Drogheda that he wouldn't be stopping for anybody, looked across at his wife and said, "Esther, we're out of petrol."

What were their options now? It was well past midnight and they were coming into the village of Castleshane, just five miles from Monaghan. "If we can push the car into Castleshane," Trevor suggested, "I'll see if Owen Mc Carville will come out and serve us some petrol to get us home."

"But Trevor, have you any money?" his wife asked, concerned. They seemed to be living constantly 'on the bread line.'

"Yes, I have a fiver," came the reply, "and that's all we need."

That was assurance enough for Esther and she joined Trevor in pushing the car the half-mile to the top of an incline from where it would run easily down to the forecourt of Owen Mc Carville's filling station.

When Trevor went up to the house, where Owen lived, it was all shut up. There wasn't a light on. The family were obviously in bed. He rang the bell and a few minutes later Owen came to the door. When Trevor explained his dilemma he gladly served them with 'a fiver's worth' of petrol.

It was two o'clock in the morning before Trevor and Esther were crawling into bed, and Trevor wouldn't have long to lie.

He had to be up early to go to work.

12

IT SOUNDS URGENT

The next day dragged.

Trevor had gone to work as usual, having passed a few restless hours in bed. Esther had stayed in bed, tossing and turning, for as long as her agitated spirit would allow. She kept wondering what was happening in the hospital in Drogheda.

How was her 'wee Monty?' That was her sole concern.

Although she longed to find out how he was, she waited until after nine o'clock in the morning before going in to Aggie, her next-door neighbour, to ask if she might use the phone.

The answer she received in response to her enquiry about Raymond's condition was that he had 'spent a comfortable night' and was 'stable.' Periodic anxious phone calls during the day elicited the same reaction from different members of staff on the ward. Raymond was always 'stable.'

Esther tried to find some crumb of consolation in the repetition of the word. If he was stable he maybe wasn't getting very much better, but he could hardly be in any danger. She was left to count the hours until Trevor arrived in from work and then they would be free to return to the hospital to see him.

It had come to five o'clock in the afternoon, and Trevor would soon be home. Esther was busy making the tea and doing a washing in an old, leaky, twin-tub machine. Trevor was to collect his sister Jacqueline from her work on his way back. She would look after Darren so that they could leave as soon as they were ready.

Just when Esther thought that everything was in order for a less nerve-racking trip to Drogheda than that of the previous day, Aggie came rushing in.

She was out of breath. "There is somebody from the hospital on the phone, Esther. They want to speak to you. It sounds urgent," she gasped.

Esther dashed in next door and picked up the phone.

"Raymond's condition has deteriorated, Mrs. Gillanders," came the message from a nurse in the children's ward. "You may come quickly."

"We are getting ready to come," Esther replied. "I'm waiting for my husband to come in from work and then we will be on our way." This explanation sounded so pathetic and paltry to her even as she spoke, given the gravity of the situation. All the alarm bells in Esther's being had begun to ring at once, and the effect was devastating.

"Well, we would ask you to come as soon as you possibly can," the voice at the other end of the line repeated, with a seriousness that was almost scary.

Aggie was right. It sounded urgent.

There was more to it than a mundane, day-to-day sense of urgency, though. This was more than, 'If you don't hurry you'll miss the bus.' Esther's instinct picked up sinister vibes. They had been suddenly catapulted, she recognised straight away, into a life-or-death situation.

In panic, Esther phoned Trevor's work, only to be informed that he had already left. She knew that there were only two other places he could possibly be. He was either out on the road in the car somewhere, or in picking up 'Jackie' from the shop where she worked. Her next move was to phone Fleming's Supermarket and ask for Jackie.

When her sister-in-law was called to the phone Esther asked her immediately, "Where's Trevor? The hospital has been on. We have to go to Drogheda at once. Raymond's condition has deteriorated."

"He's here. He has just arrived to collect me," Jackie replied, instantly appreciating the critical nature of the call. "We'll leave here at once."

When Trevor saw his sister coming down through the shop he sensed that there must be something seriously wrong. He felt a strange sickly emptiness inside. Jackie looked unusually ill at ease. There were no smiles, no cheery greeting, just a straight, anxious face. His hunch was to prove correct, as soon as she spoke.

"Trevor, we have to get home immediately," she told him. "Esther has just been on the phone. The hospital want you both up to Drogheda as soon as you can make it. There is a problem with Raymond."

They hurried out to the car and set off for the house where Esther was out waiting on the step. It was all she could think to do in the circumstances, and she had an unexpected visitor before Trevor and Jackie arrived.

It was John Lavery, Trevor's boss. Having taken Esther's call at the bakery he realised that she was deeply distressed and had called out to see if he could be of any assistance. When he came upon the agitated mother on the doorstep, John, not a man normally noted for his depth of spiritual conviction, suggested the only course of action he could think of.

"Come on in, Esther, and we'll pray," he said.

"It's too late for that, John!" Esther exclaimed, waving her arms wildly in the air in a gesture of utter desperation. "It's far too late for that!"

They were still standing outside when Trevor and his sister arrived. Trevor hurtled into the house for another flour-strewn change and Esther and he were soon ready to make a second dash for Drogheda.

John, appreciating that the young couple were both beside themselves with worry, had another offer to make. "Would you like me to take you up the road to the hospital?" he enquired. "I don't think you're in much of a state to be driving, Trevor."

"Don't worry about us, we'll be O.K., John," Trevor shouted over his shoulder as he climbed into the car. Trevor and Esther saw Raymond's illness as their own personal problem.

Many friends were very generous in their offers of help, but there were times when the young couple just wanted to be alone, to face together whatever it was that life was going to throw at them next.

There followed another hair-raising journey to the hospital. Trevor drove as hard as he could, but on automatic pilot. He wasn't thinking of what he was doing. His mind was at his destination while his body was still on the way. The hazard lights were going, producing an ominous eerie clicking inside the car. His foot was pinning the accelerator to the floor. All that mattered was that he and Esther reached Drogheda in double-quick time.

Esther sat holding on tightly, and praying. Her prayers were not for her own safety, however, although that may have been entirely appropriate, but for Raymond. The young mother who had just told John, half an hour earlier, that it was 'too late for that,' now found herself engaged in passionate prayer.

"Oh God, I know he is dying,' she began. Her trusty sixth sense had told her that. "But please let him live until I get there. I would like to hold him in my arms and see him smile at me just once more. Surely, God, that not too much to ask," she went on to plead.

When they had parked the car, Trevor and Esther ran into the hospital. The lift was empty so they jumped into it, pressed the button and were up on Raymond's floor. They then hared across the corridor and into the ward where they had left 'wee Monty' the night before. Unknown to them, a nurse had been detailed to meet them at the door and escort them in to where Raymond was. She must have been distracted by other duties, however, for the young couple arrived there unaccompanied, and unprepared for what they were about to find.

'Wee Monty' was lying where they had last seen him. But it wasn't really 'wee Monty.' His body was motionless. His spirit had gone. So had the oxygen tent. Esther reached over to touch him. His skin was still warm, but curiously unresponsive. Drawing her fingers tenderly down his cheek brought no reaction.

They were too late.

Little Raymond had died before they could reach him.

All the tension, the expectation, the disappointment, and now the realisation of the parting, had a cataclysmic effect on Esther. Tears burst out. It was like water from a geyser that had been capped for a long time, erupting in unstoppable flow.

A father who was sitting beside his sick child at a nearby bed stepped out from behind the screen curtain and whispered hoarsely, "I'm very sorry." He then disappeared as quickly as he had appeared. He had a crisis of his own to deal with.

The compassionate nurse, who should have been there to meet them on the way in, and counsel them through their ordeal, was soon on the scene.

"Would you like to come into this little side room?" she began, making her question sound more like an instruction.

Esther said nothing. She couldn't. She was in no fit state to make any kind of coherent response.

Trevor nodded, and put his arm around his heartbroken wife. This was not only a spontaneous reaction to their shared sense of ultimate anguish, but also an attempt to comfort her. It had the added more practical value of helping to guide her along behind the nurse who was making for the 'little side room.'

They had almost reached the door of the room when the nurse turned to Esther and said quite sharply, "Esther, stop that crying! You will be upsetting all the other parents!"

That command just made the devastated young mother even worse.

Her 'wee Monty,' who, along with his big brother Darren, had been the light of her and Trevor's lives for seventeen months, had just died, and the nurse was telling her to stop crying! He was gone, and she hadn't even been there to see him go or kiss him goodbye, so how on earth could she be expected to stop crying?

On reaching the sanctuary of the little consulting room the nurse told Trevor and Esther that the hospital staff were surprised at how suddenly and unexpectedly Raymond had passed away. She then asked them if there was anyone they wanted to contact and they made a short list of relatives and friends back in Monaghan whom they felt should be informed immediately. These people would, they knew, be shocked and shattered to learn of this tragic and unforeseen turn of events.

When they had made what they considered to be the most essential phone calls Trevor and Esther returned to the side of their little son's bed. The distraught mother kept leaning over to look at him. She allowed her eyes to glide slowly over every feature of his still face. She enclosed his cooling hands in her warm ones and began to rub then gently. If only she could keep him warm. How could she keep that precious body heat from draining away?

The parents' silent vigil was interrupted by the arrival in the ward of Trevor's brother Leary and his wife Anne. John Lavery had sent them out to follow Trevor and Esther. He had been very concerned for them, telling Leary and Anne, "You'd better get up the road after that pair, for they're going to kill themselves and maybe even somebody else as well!"

Not having come upon any mangled motors by the roadside, Leary and Anne had spotted Trevor's car in the hospital car park, and were further reassured to find their brother and sister-in-law alive and well. Their relief evaporated immediately when they realised that Raymond had died.

Trevor, Leary and Anne left the ward fifteen minutes later to make a second series of phone calls to members of the wider family circle in County Monaghan, leaving Esther a solitary, grief-stricken figure, by Raymond's bed.

There, alone with him, she was possessed with an almost irrepressible urge to pick up the body and run out with it. She had no idea what she planned to do even if she were successful in escaping from the hospital with 'wee Monty's' lifeless body in her arms. It would just be great to leave everybody and everything in this horrid, cruel world behind and run off into oblivion, carrying him. She would just run, and run, and run until...

Her utopia was to prove unattainable, however.

It was her husband's voice that startled her back into reality

"Look who's here, Esther," he was saying.

The traumatised mother looked up to find that her husband had returned to the bedside accompanied by another of his brothers, Ronnie, and his wife Joyce, who, on hearing of Raymond's passing, had driven straight to the hospital. Tears flowed freely as they hugged one another in a spontaneous outpouring of sorrow and sympathy.

They sat together for what seemed an age, gazing in silent, shared grief, at the still figure in the bed.

Recognising that it had become very late, Trevor leant over and whispered softly to Esther, "Do you not think that we should soon plan to head back home, pet?"

"No, Trevor, I don't want to go yet," came the woeful reply. "I don't ever want to leave. I just want to stay here with him."

It was clear that it would be some time before she could be expected to tear herself away from Raymond's side. He looked so peaceful now, as though in a permanent, settled sleep.

Time had stopped for Esther. The world around seemed irrelevant.

All she wanted to do was stay and caress the smooth skin on 'Wee Monty's' hands and face. After a few anguished hours spent looking fondly at his lifeless frame, she was overcome by a sudden burst of anger. It was directed at God. Having recalled her frantic prayers on the way up to the hospital she asked herself, "Why did God not answer my prayer?"

"Why did He not keep 'wee Monty' alive until I arrived to say goodbye?" her smouldering rage enquired.

"If He is so great and so powerful, why could He not even answer *one* single, simple prayer?"

13

I AM COMING, LORD

Esther's already heavy heart sank to rock bottom when Trevor and she arrived back at their home in Monaghan. Although it was almost midnight the road outside the house was lined with cars and she didn't need anyone to tell her why they were there. The news of Raymond's death had spread rapidly through the family circle and amongst the local community, and a phalanx of well-meaning relatives, neighbours and friends had assembled, in traditional Irish style, to tender their condolences to the bereaved parents.

The heart-broken young couple found it difficult to enter their own home because of the crowd. There seemed to be people crammed into every nook and cranny of the house that Esther had left in such a hurry just six or seven hours before. They pushed in past a sea of solemn faces. Many of those standing around in the hallway whispered words of sympathy but these bounced off Esther like hailstones off a tin roof. She had been overcome by such a trauma of grief that all her senses seemed to have gone numb. The devastated mother had been possessed by one single compelling urge as soon as the house had come in sight, and nothing else mattered at that moment.

She had to find Darren, wherever he was, and see how he had coped with the events of the past few hours.

As she pushed her way into the packed living room where the muted conversation had petered out completely when someone had muttered that 'Trevor and Esther were back,' she spotted her son coming to meet her. Little Darren had heard his mum and dads' voices in the hall and was already threading his way through the motley maze of chairs and stools in their direction.

Esther reached down to throw her arms around him as soon as she came within hugging range, but before she could say anything her three-and-a-half-year old son spoke.

"Mummy, Raymond's gone to heaven," he said.

It was so simple, yet so reassuring.

This wasn't any practised platitude from a sympathetic adult largely desensitised by ritualistic attendance at local funerals.

This was a straightforward statement of fact from the heart of a child.

"Mummy, Raymond's gone to heaven."

These were the first words to sink into Esther's grief-stricken mind since she had come into the house, and they made such a difference.

It was a most comforting thought.

Raymond's struggles were over. He was in heaven. He was at peace.

The mother enfolded her now only son in her arms and sobbed.

She wasn't alone in her sobbing either.

Darren's declaration had pierced like an arrow straight to the core of the already softened hearts around, and tears flowed freely. There was soon barely a dry eye in the house.

Rev. David Hillen arrived shortly after Trevor and Esther had returned home. He had come to express his sympathy at Raymond's passing, to bring the distraught parents what comfort he could through scripture reading and prayer, and to offer his help and advice in the arranging of the funeral.

When Trevor and Esther had moved into a quieter room where they could be alone with their minister the bereaved mother voiced a niggling concern, which had been worrying her secretly for some time. She had been aware that with Raymond's short life expectancy she was going to have to confront it sooner or later, but she had never dreamt that it would be this soon.

"I don't want Raymond to be buried," she began, self-consciously. "I just can't bear the thought of visiting a grave and wondering what kind of a state his wee body is in now. Would it be all right to have him cremated?"

"Yes, I'm sure it would," Rev. Hillen assured her. "Your undertaker could look after that for you. I have no objections to a cremation. It doesn't really matter how you dispose of the body. Raymond's soul has gone to be with the Lord. He is already in heaven. We can arrange to have a cremation, and then there will be a funeral service in the church and we will bury his ashes in the church graveyard."

Cremation... Funeral... Ashes... Graveyard.

The words sounded distressing. The prospect was daunting.

How could the devastated couple face up to the next few days?

The thought, first introduced by Darren in childlike simplicity, and then repeated by David in absolute sincerity, that Raymond was already in heaven, proved to be the only tiny chink of light in a world that had suddenly become enveloped in gloom and despair. It was a ray of hope, however tenuous, to cling to.

The following day Trevor and Esther, some close members of the family, and the baby-sitters all made the journey to Drogheda to see the body of the little one they had all loved so well, for the final time. The morgue was a chilling place in which to pay one's last respects and many of the party were mesmerised motionless and speechless when they saw the tiny seventeen-month-old frame laid out in death.

Trevor and Esther stood close together, united in the silence of utter anguish. Hankies were very much in evidence. Nobody spoke, and for a full five minutes nobody moved.

Then suddenly, unexpectedly, someone broke rank.

Jane, one of the baby-sitters, walked forward very deliberately, and bending down, kissed Raymond's pale, cold forehead. Little did the heart-broken teenager think at the time, but that simple, spontaneous act was to mean more to Esther than all the kind words of sympathy she had heard up until then. It was, she reckoned, an impromptu demonstration of genuine love and compassion.

Family members travelled to Dublin a few days later to afford comfort and support to Trevor and Esther during the cremation in Glassnevin Cemetery in the city. The tiny urn containing his ashes was then taken to Ballyalbany Presbyterian Church in Monaghan for burial the next day, Wednesday, January 19, 1983.

The church was packed well before the service was due to begin that afternoon. Those who hadn't come early were forced to stand in the porch or anywhere they could find a space.

In the course of his address Rev. Hillen referred to two verses from the Bible. He used these to illustrate how God showed His love for children, and their importance in His blueprint for the restoration of mankind to Himself.

The first of these, 'a little child shall lead them,' was from the Book of Isaiah in the Old Testament. The other was the reaction of Jesus as He rebuked His disciples for turning children away from Him. 'Let the little children come to Me, and do not forbid them; for of such is the kingdom of God,' He had commanded.

Obviously aware of the depth of sorrow in the community, and the tide of sympathy for Trevor and Esther as demonstrated by the large attendance at the funeral, Rev Hillen voiced the sentiments of many when he said, "We often find it hard to understand why these things happen." He didn't leave it there, however, but went on to give a possible solution. It was one that very few in the congregation would have contemplated, but David Hillen clearly considered it valid.

"Perhaps God is trying to break into this young family," he suggested.

Esther had begun to think that too. As their minister talked about 'a little child leading them' her mind had gone back to

Rev. Workman's message in the Hillgrove Hotel the previous autumn. Had God taken their little lamb to lead them into His fold, she wondered.

Some days earlier, when the church organist had been helping the parents choose the hymns for the service, she had asked them if they had any particular favourites they would like included. Trevor and Esther didn't know very many hymns, not having been regular in their attendance at church, but there was one, which they had heard at a mission once, that they thought they would like incorporated in the service. They liked the tune and felt somehow that it represented God calling little Raymond to be with Him in heaven.

It was, 'I hear Thy welcome voice, that calls me Lord to thee.'

Each time the congregation began to sing the chorus, which was in the form of a response to the thought expressed in the verses of the hymn, Esther joined in.

'I am coming, Lord,

Coming now to Thee," she sang, and further emphasised her intent by saying in her heart, 'Yes, Lord. I'm coming.'

What she really meant was that if coming to You, Lord, means a guaranteed ticket to the Promised Land to see my 'wee Monty' again, then I'm coming. She had little interest in, nor indeed did she fully understand the meaning of, the latter two lines of the chorus that gave the reason why anyone seeking peace and satisfaction would want to come to Jesus. It was,

'Trusting only in the blood'

That flowed on Calvary.'

She was, though, continuing to think of spiritual matters, and develop in the ease with which could communicate with God. He, unknown to Esther, was gradually breaking down all the barriers, and becoming ever more accessible to her.

At the close of the service Trevor stepped forward to pick up the urn containing the ashes of his little son and carry it tenderly outside to the church graveyard for burial.

He was overcome with emotion on that slow walk out of the church. Tears streamed down his face, and although he could see very little he was conscious that many in the large congregation were weeping too.

Later, at the graveside, Rev. Hillen spoke again as Raymond's ashes were committed to mother earth.

Trevor's thoughts were not with what David was saying, however. They were completely focused on the small urn that had just been lowered into the grave.

Gazing at it intently, through his tears, he said within his own heart, "Son, I know where you are going. But where am I going?"

14

IT'S GOOD TO COUNT THE COST

When all the busyness of the funeral had passed, Trevor, Esther and Darren were left juggling a strange mixture of emotions.

The house had become unusually quiet. There was no little Raymond to speak to, and to smile back at them, every time they passed through the living room. The eyes that had followed them around the house from their base station on the white rug in front of the fire had gone. The steady stream of visitors who had called in to express their sympathy at the time of the funeral had gradually dried up.

All three of them missed Raymond terribly and cherished their own particular and favourite memories of him. His death had left a void, an indescribable emptiness in their lives.

In another sense, however, the parents who had seen their little son so ill, and in such discomfort, so many times, were relieved that his suffering was at last at an end.

Many of those who had come to express their condolences around the time of the funeral had assured them that Raymond was now 'in a better place.' Knowing that he was in heaven continued to bring them a measure of comfort as they tried to rebuild their lives without their 'wee Monty.'

Days and weeks rolled into months and Trevor and Esther began to recognise that their experience with Raymond, and the precious nature of their memories of him, had influenced their lives in two significant ways.

The first of these was that they felt the need to fill the vacuum in their home by entering a programme of short and long term fostering. This allowed them to hear the patter of little feet, and the chatter of childish voices around the house once more, and it also provided company for Darren, whatever the length of their stay. In addition to fostering a number of children in that period Trevor and Esther also became involved with Breakaway. This was a scheme whereby mentally-handicapped children were given respite care to afford their parents, many of whom lavished twenty-four hour a day attention upon them, a break. Having learnt much through looking after Raymond, with all his specific and individual needs, they were ideally qualified for this role, and derived a great sense of satisfaction from fulfilling it.

Rev. David Hillen became a regular visitor to Trevor and Esther's home following Raymond's death, and his calls helped maintain the bereaved young couple's awareness of another immediate need in their lives. The second result of 'wee Monty's' passing was that they began to ask themselves a series of pertinent questions. These were issues they had never considered seriously before, but now with their little one having been relocated to heaven, they found themselves coming back to them, with each other, and with their minister, time and time again.

Amongst the first question that confronted David when he began calling at the house in the days immediately after the funeral was, "Why has this happened to us?" Trevor and Esther would often seek to justify this enquiry by going on to say, "We were told that Raymond could live until he was six. So why did we have to part with him after seventeen months?"

"God knew that the time had come to call him to Himself," David Hillen would explain carefully when confronted with this kind of query. "He probably saw that this little lamb had suffered enough in his fragile body and thought it best to transport him to His pain-free fold in heaven."

As the year progressed through its seasons and David continued to visit Trevor and Esther he noticed a gradual change in their attitude. Their minister displayed a genuine concern for them as a grieving young couple. This was evident in his patient responses to their many questions and his practice of reading the Bible and praying with them every time he called, and it led them into a deeper consideration of spiritual matters.

Trevor and Esther knew, having heard it in isolated mission meetings in the past, and from Rev. Hillen when opportunity arose in his recent visits, that if they were ever to join their 'wee Monty' in heaven, they needed to be saved.

David was conscious of this awakening in their minds when they began to ask about the implications of a possible conversion on their current life style.

Trevor was not a heavy drinker but he liked a bottle of beer on a Saturday night with his mates. What would he do about that if he were to come to Christ? Could he do without it, he often wondered.

The issue for Esther was different. She loved the social scene. It was the thought of possibly having to give up the partying with her friends and the occasional night out to a dance in one of the halls around the town and district that she found hard to come to terms with.

By the time a year had elapsed Trevor and Esther were asking their minister quite openly about these reservations. As David drew their attention to what the Bible taught about the importance of accepting Jesus into their lives, either one of them would be sure to ask at some stage, "If we became Christians would we have to give up all the things we enjoy? Would we have to make big changes in the way we live?"

Rev. Hillen was always very careful in replying to such an enquiry. He knew that if he said 'Yes' it would make the Christian life sound to them as though it meant following a list of rules from The Killjoy's Handbook, which it didn't. If, on the other hand, he said 'No,' it would sound as though anyone could take the name of Christ upon them and still live as they pleased, which they couldn't.

He had one carefully considered answer to this often-asked question. Regardless of which partner posed it, or how it was phrased, when the discerning minister was aware that either Trevor or Esther was thinking seriously about issues of life, death and the hope of heaven beyond, he invariably responded with, "It's good to count the cost."

Trevor had by then begun to lie awake at nights, weighing up these matters. He had secretly started to count the cost of becoming a follower of Jesus Christ. On the one hand lay the prospect of what David had described as 'peace with God in your heart in this life and the assurance of a home in heaven when you die.' On the other lay the drinks in the pub with his cronies and the nights out with Esther at the parties and dances. He had also to add to that pan on the scales that if he did become a Christian he would probably have to stand a lot of ridicule from his mates. Some of them had no time, he knew, for 'holy Joes.'

Two mental pictures haunted him. It seemed that every time he closed his eyes in the silent dark of the bedroom, in the hope of snatching a few hours sleep before his early morning rise, either one of them would come back to completely dominate his restless mind.

The first was of Raymond's look, as he had passed him that evening, all of a flurry. It was the look that had never left him. It was the look that had asked, through wordless expression, 'What is life all about?'

The other was of Ballyalbany Presbyterian Church graveyard on a darkening January afternoon. There was a crowd of people around, a shallow hole in the ground much smaller than a normal grave, and at the bottom of it lay a tiny urn, covered by a blue velvet cushion.

Trevor couldn't rid himself of these images, no matter how hard he tried. He soon recognised that sometime he was going to have to make a definite choice. The images weren't going to go away, the urge to get right with God was becoming stronger by the day, and he, as a person, was becoming increasingly discontent.

Slowly but surely Trevor had moved on from only wanting to get to heaven, whatever it cost, simply because little Raymond would be waiting for him there. He now realised that he had sinned and longed to have those sins forgiven and the peace of God in his heart.

The matter came to a head one Wednesday evening in November 1984. Esther was out at a course on foster-care in Navan, Trevor was at home and the children were in bed. When he was sure that Darren and the foster-child at that time were both sound asleep Trevor settled down to listen to some music.

One of his favourites amongst a number of the vinyl LP records he had acquired over the previous year was called 'We Thank Thee,' by Jim Reeves. As he listened to that record repeatedly he began to concentrate on two particular tracks. One of these was entitled, 'Have Thine Own Way, Lord,' and the other, 'I'd Rather Have Jesus Than Silver or Gold.' Trevor sat by the old record player and played those two pieces, over and over again. Jim Reeves' clear voice had lodged every word of each of them securely in his memory bank, and yet he still kept listening to them. Again, and again and again.

An hour passed and Trevor was still playing the same two hymns. During that time, however, he had become gripped by an overwhelming sense of his sin and guilt before God. Eventually this awareness became so overpowering that he fell to his knees at the settee in the room and pleaded with God for mercy.

His desperate prayer went something like, "Oh God, I know I'm a sinner, and I have come to confess my sins before You. I also know that Jesus died on the cross to take away my sins. Here and now I ask you, God, to forgive my sins for His sake. Please come into my heart and life and give me peace with You." It wasn't the most eloquent prayer that Trevor was to offer in his lifetime, but it was one of the most sincere, for it represented the longing cry of a penitent heart.

When he had finished praying he remained on his knees for a few minutes. It was strange. He felt mentally exhausted, emotionally drained and spiritually liberated all at once.

It was clear that something dramatic had happened.

While he had been pleading with God for peace in his soul and forgiveness from his sin, the awful sense of guilt that had been weighing him down for more than a year now, had disappeared.

It had evaporated! It was gone! He was free! It was as if all the world's troubles had been lifted off his shoulders.

Trevor rose from his knees a new man.

He felt as though he were floating in space. The pull of earth had receded and weightlessness had set in!

His sins were gone. He had come to Christ and was now His child. He was saved!

What a wonderful surprise this would be for Esther.

How he longed for her to come home.

He just couldn't wait to share this thrilling news with her!

15

WHAT ABOUT ME?

"Esther, I have something to tell you," Trevor began, as soon as he thought that his wife would be in the most receptive mood, shortly after she returned.

She was totally unaware that her husband had been looking at the clock every five minutes for the past hour and a half, willing on this moment. He had been wise enough to wait until she had hung up her coat and filed away the pamphlets she had picked up at the course before introducing the exciting news of his life-changing experience with God.

"And what's that, Trevor?" Esther replied. She thought it odd that he should preface his announcement, whatever it was about, with, 'I have something to tell you.' Trevor usually just said what he had to say, and that was it. This must be something important. Could it be about one of the children? Or maybe one of the wider family circle had phoned. She stopped what she was doing and looked at him, wondering what this was all about.

"I got saved there tonight, Esther!" he exclaimed joyfully. A broad smile creased his shining face and his eyes sparkled with the light of a new life. "I was listening to that Jim Reeves LP and I was so worried about my sin that I just knelt down at the sofa and asked God to save me. It is a tremendous feeling, Esther, just to know..."

He broke off suddenly in mid-sentence, immediately conscious that this, his first public declaration of his faith in Christ was not being received in the way he had somehow imagined it would be.

Esther, instead of looking pleased, appeared crestfallen. The exuberant Trevor was taken aback for she seemed more disappointed than delighted. He was soon to learn the reason.

"And where does that leave me now, Trevor?" was her immediate reaction. "What about me? Now that you have gone and done it, how am I ever going to be saved on my own? Didn't we already decide that we would do it together? And now you have gone on yourself and left me behind."

Trevor and she had been through so much together in the past few years that she had built up some sort of a romantic picture of how they would take the final step of faith together. There would be a mission. The hall or church would be warm and comfortable. There would a lot of people and a cosy, clinging Christian atmosphere. Soft music would be wafting in the air. Trevor and she would go forward at the end, side by side, kneel down together, and be saved at the same time...

And now he had gone and spoiled it all! He had shattered her dream! How inconsiderate and selfish!

What was she expected to do now?

Trevor's obvious joy and delight in his newly found faith and her sense of having been left behind in a momentous decision that could have a lasting impact on both of their lives, plunged Esther into a state of inner turmoil.

She reacted by proving awkward. The slightest annoyance caused her to lose her temper with Trevor. She began to argue with him with only minimal provocation. When feeling particularly spiteful she would even resort to using bad language when he was around. This was out of character for Esther but if she thought it would upset Trevor, who was floating about as though he had just taken up permanent residence on cloud nine, it would be worth it.

The galling thing was, however, that it didn't seem to be making any difference whatsoever to him. He just went on telling her how happy he was now and being as kind and considerate to her as possible. And that only made matters worse!

It was so frustrating that Trevor was saved and she wasn't.

Esther wanted to come to Christ as well. She had made up her mind that she would, shortly after Raymond's funeral. She may have sung, 'I am coming, Lord,' with her voice but not her heart, but following the discussions with Rev. Hillen she was determined to give her life to the Lord at some stage. It would be in her own way, and in her own time, however. At least that was what she thought until Trevor had gone and messed things up.

Her dad had been diagnosed with cancer in July 1983 and it seemed that there was little hope of a cure. Esther visited him often and longed to know if he was as sure of going to heaven as Rev. Hillen had told Trevor and her that true Christians could be.

When sitting by his bedside in February 1984 she knew that the end was near and was desperate to ask him, "Daddy, are you saved?" She couldn't though. The words, which were in her mind, refused to come out of her mouth.

Instead, she was gripped by an arresting and sobering thought. What right have you, it asked, to be concerned about another man's soul, even if that other man is your own father, when you are not concerned with your own?

Esther rushed out of the bedroom in floods of tears.

Her daddy was dying, and she felt helpless to ask him the question she was sure he needed to hear, because she couldn't give a positive answer to it herself. And that was to be her final opportunity to ask it.

It was the last time she was to see her dad alive, for he passed away the following day. One of the hymns that were sung at his funeral lived with her for weeks. It was, 'Will Your Anchor Hold In The Storms Of Life?' Esther soon began to realise that her anchor wasn't holding. In fact, she didn't have an anchor at all.

Now, ten months on from her father's death, and with the memory of her conviction at his bedside still plaguing her from time to time, Trevor's confident confession of faith had brought her face to face with her need of salvation once more. She had stopped worrying about missing out on a few nights out with her friends. Since Trevor had become a Christian he appeared to have totally lost interest in the social scene. All he wanted to do was read his little New Testament, every spare moment he had.

Three days after Trevor's conversion, Esther, who was still in a state of mental and spiritual anguish, was walking through the hall of their Monaghan home.

Suddenly she heard a voice speaking to her. It was so plain that she was startled and stopped in mid-step.

"Esther," it said. "You have been counting the cost too long. Have you ever considered how much it cost Me?"

The voice had come as a bolt from the blue. Then the truth of something that she already thought she knew hit her with unexpected force. She was left staggering spiritually when she considered its personal application.

It had cost God His only Son. It had cost Jesus His very life. All in order that she might go free.

Esther rushed up the stairs and into a bedroom. She fell down on her knees at the side of the bed and began pouring out her heart to God, praying that He would forgive her sins, and also forgive her for taking so long to come to Him.

"Lord, Jesus, I realise now how much it cost You to provide salvation for me," she burst out, her rebellious spirit broken. "I believe You died on the cross for me and I want to trust You now. Thank You, Jesus, for taking my sins away. Please come into my life and change me and be my Saviour and help me to live for You. Amen."

When she pulled herself up to her feet again, Esther knew that she was different. The sense of anger, and guilt and frustration had all gone. And now, she could hardly believe it, instead of dreaming up a series of niggling little annoyances to test her husband's Christian patience to the absolute limit, she could hardly wait for him to come home to tell him that she had also asked Jesus to come into her heart.

Esther had undergone a miraculous transformation in those few moments she had spent on her knees by that bed. She had, in fact, knelt down as a child of the devil and risen as a child of God.

Later that day, when Trevor came in from work, his wife was waiting for him. This time, though, it wasn't to greet him with some trivial complaint, accompanied by an unnecessary swear word or two. It was now the turn of her face to glow, and eyes to gleam as she enquired softly, "Can you guess what happened to me today, Trevor?"

"No, I can't Esther," her husband replied. As he looked into her face he knew it must be something good, but it would be interesting to hear just what.

"I was saved. I asked Jesus to come into my heart up in the bedroom this morning," she told him, with great pleasure.

"That's wonderful, Esther!" Trevor exclaimed at once. Then reaching over to give her a huge hug of joy and relief, he went on, " I have been praying that you would come to faith in Christ as well. Now we both belong to Him!"

It was fantastic news. They were 'one in Christ Jesus,' as his New Testament described it.

"Just one thing, though," Esther said an hour our two later. "I don't want you to tell anybody about what I did today. For a while at least, to see how it goes."

Trevor was euphoric at her confession of salvation and she didn't want him spreading it all round the town.

The new convert had two reasons for imposing this broadcasting restriction. The first was that she just wanted to be sure that she 'had done it right,' and was 'truly saved.' The other was that she didn't want to have to make too big a change in her lifestyle. She wanted to hold on to her old friends if she could. It would be marvellous if she could enjoy the best of both worlds, and she wouldn't have to endure the taunts of those who would probably laugh at her for 'turning good-livin''

She wanted to be 'a secret disciple.'

But would it work?

16

THE HALF-BISCUIT TIN

"Have you a bigger lunch-box you could give me, Esther?" Trevor enquired one morning as his wife was starting to prepare his lunch for the day.

"Whatever would you want that for?" Esther replied, answering his question with one of her own. She was surprised at this request and, afraid that her husband was not satisfied with what she had been giving him, went on to add, "Am I not giving you enough for your lunch, love?"

"No. It's nothing like that," he reassured her hastily. "My idea is that if I had a bigger lunch-box I could put my New Testament in the bottom of it and read it over my lunch break."

Trevor was hungry, but it wasn't for more sandwiches.

He had developed an insatiable appetite for the scriptures, and God had challenged him to carry his New Testament to work.

When Esther began sending him out, two days later, not with his old plastic lunch-box, but with his sandwiches in a half-biscuit tin, he was delighted. The truth was that he had a burning desire to read his New Testament in the lunch-break, but was slightly afraid of his workmates in the bakery seeing him at it, in case they would think he had 'gone soft.' The half-biscuit tin was the answer. When eating alone he placed the New Testament in the bottom of the box and read away. If, however, anyone came uncomfortably close he merely slid the lid over a few inches to obscure its contents.

Gradually, though, as he became spiritually more nourished and strengthened by the Bread of Life, he found himself less concerned about his mates seeing him immersed in the Word of God. What the Lord had done in his life had begun to work its way out. It was irrepressible and unmistakeable.

The singing of choruses to himself as he worked was another indicator to all in the bakery that 'a change had come over' Trevor. He couldn't keep himself from singing one that he had heard in Rev. Sam Workman's mission, two years before.

It was, 'He lives, He lives,

Christ Jesus lives today!'

The last two lines of that chorus meant so much to him, for they expressed exactly how he felt.

'You ask me how I know he lives,

He lives within my heart!' he would sing with complete conviction.

A few months after his conversion, and having spotted the New Testament in the half-biscuit tin and heard the choruses and verses from hymns that Trevor had started to sing as he worked around the bakery, the other staff would nod and smile knowingly at one another.

"Gillanders has turned all religious, " they would say now and again. They even joked about taking a bet to see 'how long he could keep it.'

Another way in which Trevor chose to make a public statement of his faith in Christ was by carrying the new Bible, which Esther had bought him, to church. Rev. Hillen was delighted to have Trevor, who had been irregular in his attendance at the services in Ballyalbany until recently, coming out on every possible occasion. Not only did he never miss a Sunday morning but he also started to attend the midweek Praise, Prayer and Bible Study session. He simply couldn't learn enough about the Bible and the Christian life. It was all so new, so fresh, and so thrilling!

It was in the Sunday morning service that Trevor found it the greatest challenge to open his Bible and follow the reading when the minister announced his sermon text for the day. Very few others carried a Bible to church as he did, and with the Sunday morning congregation invariably the biggest of the week Trevor felt that every eye in the church was turned in his direction as the pages of his Bible rustled. This momentary attention, whether real or imagined, made Trevor feel somewhat self-conscious but he continued to carry and consult his Bible, for he considered it an appropriate means of making a public declaration of his faith.

Now that Esther was saved, and despite her wish to keep her salvation a secret, she began to read the Bible and pray every day. She was expecting her third child at the time and one of her most frequent observations to her Heavenly Father, with whom she was now on regular speaking terms, was, "Lord, I so much want this baby to be a boy."

Her wish was fulfilled when their third son, Gregory, was born in January 1985. What a delight to have another baby boy to cuddle, but Esther, the young Christian, was to experience a few extremely anxious days after his birth. Baby Gregory, who had been born five weeks earlier than expected, had acute breathing problems. Although these settled down fairly quickly, it became obvious, some days later, that he was heavily jaundiced.

As his condition didn't appear to be responding to treatment the medical staff in Monaghan decided that he would be best moved to Drogheda Hospital where specialist help was available. Since Esther was also unwell following the birth, she was unable to travel with him. This meant that she was forced to watch as the ambulance men wheeled yet another of her babies out to their waiting vehicle in a specially designed incubator.

Esther cried as the incubator disappeared down the corridor. It was heart-breaking, for it brought back so graphically the number of times little Raymond had to be rushed to Drogheda, in his valiant, but ultimately unsuccessful, struggle to survive.

Baby Gregory's desperately worried mother was now equipped with a source of inner strength and comfort that she didn't have in those days, however. Although she had uttered a few panic prayers over that trying time, these had been inspired more by frustration than faith. Now she was convinced that she was getting through to God, and that her petitions were being accorded immediate attention, every time she prayed.

Trevor and she were having their faith tested but they both prayed earnestly for their little baby and three days later they were able to bring him home and introduce him to big brother Darren.

When he was just a few months old, Gregory took ill once more, and was treated with a course of antibiotics. This, in its turn, caused an allergic reaction which became evident when the infant's mouth and throat broke out in a distressing attack of thrush.

Their former experience of this malady was now set to cause Trevor and Esther some heart-searching. As Esther sat by her baby's cot in the middle of the night she thought back to when Raymond had thrush, and how it had been cured, almost immediately, with a charm.

Gregory's mouth and throat were now in such a state that he couldn't bear to take food of any kind. It was far too painful. So little Gregory soon became very hungry. A visit to the man with the charm could probably put him out of his agony within hours. It was a big temptation for Trevor and Esther, when they witnessed their little son in such misery.

This time, though, they refrained. An extra spiritual dimension, which had come free with their new nature, which had come as a result of their new birth, told them that there was something 'not right' about the use of charms. It was difficult, but they persisted with the doctor's medicine, and in prayer, and Gregory recovered in less than a fortnight.

In the spring of 1985 Trevor and Esther realised that their social interest and outlook had changed. They needn't have worried about 'having to give up' their partying or Saturday night drink in the pub. They discovered that these things no longer held any fascination for them. Their appeal had gone.

Trevor and Esther found it much more rewarding to spend any spare time they had in visiting people whom they knew to be Christians. One such couple was Trevor's uncle Andy and aunt Edna. The four of them, two recent converts, and a pair of more mature Christians, really relished being together. They had so much in common now that they didn't have before.

Andy and his wife had gathered from Esther's conversation that she was now a believer although she had never told them so, in so many words. She had found it easy enough to keep her 'secret,' for with two young children of her own, and one of them just a baby, plus the foster children, she was hardly ever out of the house. Not like Trevor, who was always out and about, but had come to the point where he didn't care who knew about his salvation. He was just bubbling over with it.

One evening, as they were all sitting chatting around the fire Trevor raised the subject of his personal unease at his continued membership of the freemasons. His uncle told him that he had once been 'a mason' too, but had resigned his membership after his conversion. He also lent his concerned nephew a book entitled, 'Christ, the Christian and Freemasonry,' by W.J. Mc Cormick. Before Trevor left for home that night his uncle advised him to 'read the book carefully and consider the whole matter prayerfully.'

Having read the book, and prayed long and hard about the issue, as had been suggested, Trevor recognised that he also needed to come out of the freemasons. The next time they met Trevor solicited uncle Andy's help in drafting a letter of resignation.

When this was complete, to both their satisfaction, and posted, Trevor was relieved. He felt 'free' in the true sense of the word. It reminded him of a verse he had read in his New Testament, just a week or two before. Speaking to some of his Jewish followers, Jesus had declared, "If the Son makes you free, you will be free indeed."

Not only had Trevor and Esther begun to seek out and enjoy Christian company, but when a gospel mission was held in Monaghan in May they started to attend as often as possible. If a baby-sitter was available they went together, otherwise either of them would go on his or her own.

One afternoon during the mission Esther called in at her sister-in-law Anne's house and Trevor's sister Caroline happened to be there.

As they were having a cup of tea around the kitchen table Caroline said, "I heard that there was somebody saved at the meeting last night." Then, turning to look over at her sister-in-law, continued, "And what's more, Esther, I heard that it was you."

"That's a very strange thing, Caroline," Esther replied with a smile, well aware that her moment of truth had come. "It couldn't have been me. I have been saved for six months."

"You don't mean it, Esther! Is that right?" Caroline exclaimed in amazement.

"Oh, yes. You'd better believe it, for it's right enough," Esther assured her. "I came to the Lord a few days after Trevor, but I just haven't told very many people yet."

Now that Caroline and Anne had both heard the news of Esther's conversion it wasn't long until they had told other members of the family and some of their friends. Esther may have succeeded in 'not telling many people' for six months, but from that moment on the news spread far and wide.

This public affirmation of her faith in Christ had an unexpectedly positive effect on Esther. As soon as she had told Anne and Caroline about the morning she had trusted Christ a tremendous sense of peace and joy flooded her soul. All the doubts vanished in an instant.

She was sure now that she 'had done it right.'

She was certain that she was 'truly saved.'

It was now all out in the open, and soon Trevor and Esther were attending every mission meeting within travelling distance from their home, witnessing to as many as would listen to them, and reading the Bible together as a family at home.

Later that year they experienced a crowning joy to their salvation.

One November morning, as Esther was helping Darren to prepare to go out to school, the six-year-old said to her, "Mummy, I would like to be saved."

"Ach would you, pet?" his mum replied, fighting to hold back a tear. "Would you like to be saved now?"

"Yes. Mummy, I would," Darren went on, the serious look on his face an outward sign of the earnest desire of his heart.

Then, forgetting about preparation, about school, and about all the hundred and one tasks she had planned to attend to that morning, Esther sat down beside her little son and told him simply how he could come to Jesus. Darren accepted the Saviour into his heart, and his mum was overjoyed. She had just pointed her first soul to the Lord! And it was her own little son!

When the children in his school class were telling their teacher their 'news' that day, Darren volunteered the information, "Miss, I got saved this morning."

"Oh that's good, Darren," teacher remarked, before going on to listen to another pupil. "I hope it makes you a better boy."

Darren was slightly disappointed at his teacher's reaction, for although he didn't feel a much 'better boy, he was certainly a much happier boy. And he was soon to be encouraged by how his news was received by others.

It transported his mum and dad up onto a higher plane of spiritual bliss, started waves of joy rippling amongst the local Christian community, and caused a stir among the angels in heaven.

17

WHATEVER YOU HAD HAS GONE

With Esther having been transformed, almost overnight, from a secret disciple to a fearless witness, and Trevor as exuberant about his faith as ever, the pair of them soon became openly active in the Christian scene in Monaghan.

Trevor continued to attend the midweek Praise, Prayer and Bible Study meeting in church. A friend had loaned him Matthew Henry's commentary on the Bible and he was soon an enthusiastic participant in the discussions on the Book of Revelation. He had also been invited to teach a Sunday School class in Ballyalbany Presbyterian Church and become a leader in its Youth Fellowship. Esther and he both had begun to help in the Faith Mission Young People's Fellowship and engage in evangelical outreach around the town. As this work expanded, and others gradually became involved, the spiritually on-fire young couple established a regular prayer meeting, with the specific focus on praying for local outreach, in their home.

Then, just as things appeared to be going well, with their joy in the Lord abounding, and their confident confirmation of their Christian faith beginning to make its mark on others, they suffered what seemed to be a setback.

It all began so simply.

Trevor and Esther were sitting at a meal in a hotel, at the reception following a family wedding, when Trevor dropped a fork. He picked it up. Then promptly dropped it again.

He was having difficulty in holding the knife, too, but the fork had become almost impossible. It was as though his hands didn't want to work any more.

This was worrying, coming as it did, after Trevor had begun to experience problems with his speech. Both he and Esther had noticed that for the previous three or four months he was having trouble articulating some words. They had both tried to ignore it in the hope that it was just a temporary impediment, which would go away through time.

It didn't, though, and Trevor found it even more annoying to discover that there was one particular word he was having exceptional difficulty in uttering. There were times when he was almost afraid to try and say the word, it was so hard to get out, and yet it was one which had become an essential element of his everyday vocabulary. He used it at home with Esther and in Sunday School and church, in conversation with others as often as he could, and in audible scripture reading and prayer.

It was the name 'Jesus.'

Soon after the fork-dropping incident, and with his speech problem becoming progressively worse and other minor malfunctions beginning to manifest themselves in different parts of his body, Trevor decided to seek medical advice.

The family doctor listened to his description of the symptoms he was experiencing and, after she had examined him, enquired if there was any history of multiple sclerosis in the family. The words came as a shock to Trevor, but 'as nothing could be confirmed until a series of tests had been carried out,' the doctor referred him to a specialist in Monaghan General Hospital.

When Trevor went for his appointment, the specialist sent him to Dublin for a CT scan, and arranged for him to have a lumbar puncture in Monaghan.

While still in hospital, having had his lumbar puncture, but before the results of it had come through, a junior doctor took Trevor into a little counselling room one day. He had been given the job of passing on the bad news. Considering the results of the tests that had already been conducted, there was, he said, a strong likelihood that Trevor had multiple sclerosis.

This diagnosis threw the energetic Christian husband and father into an immediate state of mental and spiritual anguish. When he returned to the relative silence of the ward his mind was in a whirl.

All his plans for the future had suddenly become overshadowed by the haunting image of an out-of-work baker in a wheelchair. What would happen to Esther and the family when it came to that stage, he wondered? And from what he had heard of the disease it would probably become even more debilitating than that. Who was going to look after him then?

He found the entire prospect distressing. The diagnosis had come as a sharp shock to the system.

Then there was the spiritual aspect of his life to be considered as well. He and Esther had discussed how they could make best use of their lives for God. Where did this leave him now?

As the afternoon wore on Trevor became even more agitated. Nothing seemed to make sense any more. The future looked very bleak.

Suddenly, in an outburst that was half-prayer and half-promise, Trevor cried out in utter frustration, "Lord, if You get me out of this I'll shout Your Name from the rooftops!"

When he was discharged from hospital the next day Trevor contacted John King, a local Christian leader, and told him the disturbing news. He asked John to pray, and request others to pray, that either he would be healed, or that God would reveal to Trevor the Divine plan for his life.

Despite the prognosis, and an expected gradual deterioration in Trevor's condition, Esther and he continued to attend all the meetings they possibly could. The disconcerting diagnosis had done nothing to dampen their faith in God, although it had caused them some heart-searching as to the direction of their lives.

They were at a prayer meeting one evening when Margaret, the sister of an Elim pastor, came along with a specific message for Trevor. It was from her brother, and the gist of it was, 'The Lord has revealed to me that you should hang in there and keep trusting. He is planning to use you in a mighty way for His glory, and the Devil doesn't like it. This is an attack of Satan and you must pray definitely against it.'

At that time Trevor was reading through the Epistle of James, in his personal devotions, and in the last chapter he came across a passage that startled him. It was something he didn't know was in the Bible, but surely it applied specifically to his situation.

It said, 'Is anyone among you sick? Let him call for the elders of the church, and let them pray over him, anointing him with oil in the name of the Lord. And the prayer of faith will save the sick, and the Lord will raise him up...'

Trevor was excited. He showed the verse to Esther, saying, "I'm going to tell David about that verse on Sunday, and ask him if the elders would do that for me."

He had found it hard to wait until Sunday morning, and as he was leaving the church after the service he said to Rev. Hillen, with whom he had become very friendly since his conversion, "David, I have just discovered a couple of verses in James chapter five, where it says that if anybody is sick they can call the elders of the church and ask them to pray over him, and the Lord will raise him up. Can you arrange for the elders here to do that for me?"

David Hillen didn't hesitate. "Yes, Trevor, I know the verses," he replied at once. "And yes, I can fix it for the elders to pray with you. We will do it at the Praise, Prayer and Bible Study meeting on Thursday night."

When Thursday came Trevor and Esther secured the services of a baby-sitter and both of them went out to the midweek meeting. They had thought that perhaps the elders would pray for Trevor after the others had gone, but when they arrived they found that they were mistaken. That was not to be how it was going to be done.

Trevor was invited to come forward and sit on the chair which had already been placed in the centre of the floor. David and three of the church elders then stepped forward and laid their hands on him. All four of them stood around the chair as David prayed that Trevor would be healed of the infirmity which had already begun to afflict his body.

There was nothing dramatic about the procedure. It represented simply what the Bible said it should be, a 'prayer of faith.' Having prayed for Trevor, at his request, the elders and minister returned to their normal seats and Trevor went back beside Esther, and the meeting continued in its normal format.

When he awoke the next morning Trevor felt better, and within days the symptoms which had been making life increasingly difficult for him, and worrying him accordingly, had begun to disappear. Although pleased at this positive development neither Trevor nor Esther thought it strange, or even miraculous, at first.

It was merely what they had expected to happen. Such was their faith that if it said it in the Bible, then it happened. If you were told to do it in the Bible, then you did it. Since they had become children of God they had learnt to trust Him implicitly for everything. He was their Father, Friend and Supreme Counsel all rolled into one and His Word was their law. There could be no other.

Some time later Trevor was driving along the North Road in Monaghan when he was conscious that the driver in the car behind had tooted the horn at him and was now flashing the lights. On looking in his rear-view mirror he discovered that it was David Hillen. Assuming that he had some important message for him Trevor pulled in at the next opportunity. David drove in and stopped behind him.

As the two men got out of their cars and began walking towards each other, David, who had obviously something on his mind, was the first to speak. "I was driving behind you there for a while, Trevor," he began, with a warm smile, "and I just thought, isn't it wonderful what God can do? Look at you. You are an answer to prayer."

"Yes, David. It is indeed marvellous what God can do." Trevor responded enthusiastically. "Every day I live I am coming to appreciate something new about Him. His love, His power, His grace, His provision, it just goes on and on..."

Thus began an impromptu praise session on the forecourt of a garage!

Trevor's consultant was also beset with a sense of wonderment, verging on bewilderment, when his patient arrived for his next check-up.

Having examined Trevor, listened to him speak, and pored over the results of blood and other tests he remarked at length, "This is strange, but all I can say, and conclude from what I have before me, is that whatever it was that you had has gone!"

The prayer of faith had brought healing to the sick.

And medical evidence could do nothing but confirm it.

18

I CAN DO NOTHING WITH HER, LORD

Interaction with other Christians proved to have practical as well as spiritual benefits for Trevor and Esther as they found when they decided to have a couple of rooms decorated at home.

After a meeting one evening Trevor was chatting to Tom Wilson, who had taught him years before in Sunday School, and he asked him, casually, "Do you know of anybody who could do a bit of decorating for us, Tom?"

"I do indeed, Trevor," Tom replied at once. "I would think Garry Tutty's your man. He has just moved to Monaghan recently from his home in Wicklow, to help in the running of his uncle's business. He hasn't got to know many of the people round here yet and it would be good for him to meet some of the local Christians."

A few days later Trevor and Esther acted on Tom's recommendation and made contact with Garry. He agreed to undertake their wallpapering job, and on the first evening he came

Trevor was practising his guitar and singing in a nearby room.

As they were having a cup of tea together when Garry had finished work for the evening, the home decorator remarked casually, "I hear you play the guitar, Trevor."

"I do," came the reply. "At least I strum at it now and again. I enjoy learning to play and sing new hymns and choruses."

"I play and sing a bit too," Garry said. "I must say I liked some of that stuff you were playing tonight."

"Do you have a guitar?" Trevor was anxious to know.

"Aye, I do," Garry told him.

"Great. Why don't you bring it down with you the next night you are coming and we will have a session together?" Trevor suggested.

Garry was quite happy to take Trevor up on his invitation and their first practice night marked the beginning of a genuine Christian friendship.

After they had been practising together for a few months they were invited to sing in the Monaghan Christian Fellowship one Sunday evening. As there were no evening services in most of the churches in the town, many of the local Christians welcomed the opportunity to go along to the Fellowship, which met in 'The Hall' on the North Road.

Favourable reports about this new singing duo soon spread amongst the Christian community in the area and it wasn't long before Garry and Trevor were being asked to take meetings in the surrounding counties. Garry was already accustomed to speaking at meetings and he encouraged his friend and singing partner to tell of how God had intervened in his life. This was to prove beneficial to Trevor in more ways than one, for not only did it help increase his confidence in public speaking, but it also brought him into contact with many fine people in The Faith Mission.

With an increasing joint participation in the presentation of the Gospel, both in word and song, Trevor and Garry began to seek guidance from God as to how they should proceed in Christian work. This had become such a dominant issue in their lives that they began to meet at half-past six in the morning, two mornings a week, to pray.

They were concerned to petition God's help in the meetings they had been invited to conduct in the foreseeable future and also His will for their long-term involvement in the service of the Lord.

The challenge for Trevor came at the Monaghan Missionary Convention. This annual event was organised by Lucy Dudgeon and the Monaghan Christian Fellowship and was both eagerly anticipated and well attended by many Christians in 'the border counties.'

The speaker at one of the convention meetings was a representative from the World Evangelistic Crusade (WEC). As Trevor listened to what he had to say he was impressed, not only by his message but also by the way in which he put it across. His presentation was so gracious that it somehow enhanced the thought-provoking and soul-stirring nature of his address.

Trevor sat there captivated.

He was gripped by an unexpected sense of destiny.

As the speaker continued Trevor had a vivid mental flashback to an event that had occurred some months before... He was lying in a bed in Monaghan General Hospital, and was devastated to have been informed that 'there was a strong possibility' that he had multiple sclerosis. In the ensuing emotional and spiritual struggle he had spelt out the terms of a deal he had been attempting to do with God. It was, 'if You get me out of this, I'll shout Your name from the rooftops.'

That promise crashed back to smash into him like a hammer-blow as he sat listening to the speaker present a series of challenges in relation to Christian service. God had kept His side of the bargain. There could be no doubt about that. He had seen Trevor discharged from hospital, back to his wife, his family and everyday life and had cured him completely of 'whatever it was that he had.'

Had he, though, honoured his end of the contract, which he himself had proposed? Did speaking and singing God's praise to small audiences of mainly Christian people in isolated country mission halls fulfil the terms of the vow he had made? Could it honestly be described as 'shouting the name of the Lord from the rooftops?'

Trevor was so overcome by a sense of remorse at not having kept the solemn promise he had made to God, and so challenged to make his life count for Him, that he determined if the speaker made an appeal at the close of the meeting he would definitely respond. He would have no problem either nodding his head or raising his hand to affirm his heartfelt commitment to a life of dedicated Christian service.

His heart dropped, however, when he heard the kind of appeal he made. Having announced the closing hymn, 'Wash me O Lamb of God, wash me from sin,' from the Songs of Victory hymnbook, the speaker went on to add, "I believe God has been dealing very definitely with someone here tonight. If He has, and You feel Him calling you into a more committed witness for him, I want you to make your way up to the front of the hall as we sing this hymn."

This wasn't quite what Trevor had expected. The appeal wasn't going to be a lift your head or your hand job. It was going to require total body and soul participation. Trevor struggled desperately with it.

There were five verses in the hymn and the congregation had begun singing the third one, but still he hadn't moved. The pressure was beginning to mount. He could barely read the words of the hymn for his book was jerking up and down so fiercely. His hands were shaking uncontrollably.

At the start of the fourth verse he was still rooted to the spot. There were over two hundred people in First Monaghan Presbyterian Church Hall for that meeting and Trevor was sure that every single one of them knew him. What would they think of him if he went up to the front? Perhaps he should just...

As the people around him began singing the final verse Trevor felt God saying to him very clearly, 'If you want all that I have for you, then you must respond. Now.'

In that instant Trevor decided that he was left with no choice but to respond, so he determined to make his way up to the front as discreetly as possible. He would slip up silently, and then perhaps very few would notice.

Not for the first time that evening, however, things didn't work out just as Trevor had hoped. As he was leaving the row of seats in which he was sitting, on his furtive journey to the front, he caught his foot on a vacant chair near the aisle, and in pulling away from it caught on another one. There was, what he imagined to be, an almighty clatter. Eyes were raised from hymnbooks and a hundred or more heads turned in his direction.

By the time Trevor had made it to the front of the hall every single person in it knew that he was there, despite all his scheming!

It didn't worry him by then, though.

He had responded to a call, which he was certain had come from God, and had no regrets.

Wesley Lindsay, one of the WEC team at the convention, moved over beside Trevor, and as the congregation filed from the hall, spoke to him in relation to serving the Lord in the future. God had, he was convinced, put His hand on Trevor's life and would bless him in every aspect of his work in preaching the Gospel and teaching the scriptures.

When he arrived home, half an hour later, Trevor told Esther about his struggle at the seat, his going forward during the appeal and his personal commitment to God and His service.

"I am quite sure that God is calling me to work for Him," he said, when coming to the end of his summary of the evening's events. "And I really feel that before I set out on a personal ministry I ought to go to Bible College. There are so many things that I need to learn."

Esther knew her husband well enough to realise that he meant business on this matter. She also recognised, with Wesley, that 'God had put His hand' on his life.

The problem was, He hadn't done that for her.

Her reaction to his proposal was that of the dutiful Christian wife. "That's O.K., Trevor," she was prepared to venture. "You go to Bible College and prepare to serve the Lord. I will stay at home, look after the boys, find a job, and support you in every way that I possibly can."

It was commendable, but not complete, as far as Trevor was concerned. "Thanks, Esther," he replied. "But I want you to come too. I wouldn't feel like going away and leaving you, so I won't be going without you."

"No, love," was his wife's firm decision. "I don't feel that I'm ready for that. God has called you. Not me. I'm just a housewife, and happy to be one."

This was a downer for Trevor. He was sure that he had been called of God. Esther was sure that she hadn't.

Having raised the subject with her a few times only to meet with the same unsatisfactory to him, 'you go, and I'll stay,' response, Trevor went to a local Faith Mission worker, Elsie Moynan, for advice. When he had recounted his concerns to her she told Trevor that all he could do was pray. It would be wrong to attempt to force Esther into going to Bible College, merely to keep him company. Only the call of God could change her mind, she counselled.

Still absolutely convinced that God wanted him to go to Bible College, and then serve Him with his life, but unwilling to embark upon any of this without Esther by his side, Trevor began taking his 'burden to the Lord.' And all he could do was 'leave it there.'

"I can do nothing with her, Lord," he would pray often, in a mild exasperation arising from frustrated spiritual ambition. "I'm leaving her up to You."

19

HOW AM I GOING TO TELL HIM?

If Trevor continued to insist that he wasn't going to Bible College without his wife, he certainly wouldn't be there in the near future. That much was quite clear. He began to accept this fact rather reluctantly, and continued to travel to other more distant locations, preaching and singing with Garry.

Meanwhile, back at home, Esther had identified what she considered to be a most pressing priority. Her husband's heart sank when she chose an appropriate moment to mention it to him one evening.

"You know, Trevor," she began, "we badly need this house done up." Having introduced the subject, and without giving him a chance to make any immediate response, she proceeded to itemise all the 'improvements' she had been 'thinking about.' It struck Trevor that she must have been 'thinking about' them for days, for nobody could have compiled a list that length on the spur of the moment!

Although appreciating both what she was saying and how commendable it was in a wife to keep a comfortable home, Trevor's initial reaction was to oppose such a comprehensive revamp. Although forced to agree that certain rooms would certainly benefit from a 'bit of touching up' he felt ill disposed to the prospect of refurbishment for a couple of reasons, one practical, the other spiritual.

Firstly, a makeover on the scale Esther was planning, with papering and painting in two or three rooms, fitted wardrobes in their bedroom, and new carpets throughout, would cost a lot of money. And the truth was that they didn't have a lot of money. They had just come to the stage where all their bills were paid up to date, and they could about manage to keep out of debt, provided they watched every penny. There was no way, though, that they had a few thousand punts to spare on a major programme of modernisation.

Trevor was able to put that point to Esther, but he kept his second reservation to himself. It was to do with his wish to go to Bible College, and left him with a sense of disappointment. This was not a financial matter which could be sorted out by a visit to a bank manager. It was a spiritual matter and could only be sorted out by God. If Esther was planning to 'do up' the house she mustn't have taken what he had told her about wanting to go to Bible College, but not wanting to go without her, too seriously, he reckoned. Training for Christian service would be nothing more that a distant, but impossible dream, if all Esther could think about was carpets and curtains, wallpaper and wardrobes.

Months passed, and with no prospect of any immediate change in the situation Trevor went on working in the bakery, singing at meetings, and praying that God would 'work on Esther's heart.'

That particular heart would require a lot of working on, however, for it was still set on a complete refurbishment of their home. Trevor recognised this, and as she kept insisting that the improvements she was proposing were really necessary he gave in and secured a loan to have them carried out.

Garry, who had become a daily visitor in Trevor and Esther's home helped with the decorating of the house and the putting in of the central heating. Trevor and he did as much of the practical work on all the various aspects of the revamp as possible, themselves. Nor were they the only workmen about the place. There were dozens of them, each doing his little bit to help Esther's long considered, and often talked about plans, materialize.

By the time they had finished, six months later, the house had been redecorated from top to bottom and central heating and a new fireplace had been installed. There were also fitted wardrobes in the main bedroom and carpets on all the floors, both upstairs and down. Outside, and as a marker for a possible stage two in the Esther Redevelopment Plan, foundations had been laid for an extension to the kitchen.

It was all coming together just as she had imagined.

Then one morning in late March 1989 Trevor's patient, persistent, and what he often considered in his more faithless moments to be pointless, prayers, were unexpectedly answered.

The children had only a few more days to do at school before Easter and were looking forward to the holidays. Having left them safely in the care of their respective teachers Esther was on her way home in the car. It was a lovely spring morning, full of bursting buds and birdsong, and Esther was listening to one of her favourite tapes as she drove along.

Although she had heard the tape of Keith Green hundreds of times she never seemed to tire of it and was enjoying it again that morning. As she approached the house one particular track caught her attention in a dramatic way. Up until then it had all been a pleasurable, spring-morning, easy-listening, spiritually-soothing experience. The words of the songs had been flowing over her without making any significant impression.

Now, though, a verse from the song drilled its way into the heart for which Trevor had been praying for nearly two years.

The words came like an electric shock. They were,

'Jesus commands you to go,
It should be the exception if you stay.
No wonder we're moving so slow,

If God's children refuse to obey.'

Esther pulled the car in at the kerb outside their house and played the song over again. Then again. And again.

With the message of the verse pricking her conscience Esther began an impromptu conversation with God.

"But I am the exception," her unyielding will contended.

"Tell me how?" God seemed to reply.

"Well, Trevor's a youth leader in the church," she returned.

"But what do you do?" God wanted to know.

"Trevor's a Sunday School teacher as well," Esther continued.

"And what do you do?" came the Divine response.

"Trevor is out nearly every night of the week at a meeting somewhere," she maintained resolutely.

"I'm not asking you about Trevor, though," the voice of God persisted. "All I would really like to know is, what do *you* do?"

"Well, Lord, I make the tea," she conceded, falteringly.

It sounded so absolutely pathetic as soon as she had said it. God had saved her and given her more peace in her heart and in her home that she had ever known. Her husband was actively involved in an endless round of Christian outreach.

And what was she doing for the Lord?

Answer, making the tea!

Esther's resistance was overcome, for at that moment she realised that God was calling her, personally, into some other sphere of service for Him.

Sitting there in the car, outside her home, she used the words of the song to which she had just been listening, to make a lifelong commitment.

"Yes, Lord. If You are commanding me to go, then I'll go."

It was a bold, heartfelt pledge, and its sincerity was about to be put to the test.

As soon as Esther opened the front door of her house she was met by the smell of fresh paint. Walking up the hall her feet sank into soft new carpet. The house was warm, for the central heating had just gone off. Upstairs she went to tidy away some clothes into the brand new built-in wardrobes. They, too, still had a refreshingly clean look about them.

Everything Esther's heart had ever desired was in that home. She had been planning, and then working, first on Trevor, and then latterly with a variety of tradesmen to make it what it had become. It was her dream home.

Now, though, it meant nothing to her. Its attraction had suddenly faded into insignificance. If the God who had transformed her life was calling her 'to go' what did a few tables or chairs, carpets or wardrobes matter? Everything around her had begun to appear in its true and transient nature. She had now become involved in everlasting issues.

Her mind was made up, and her soul was at peace.

How, though, was she going to tell Trevor? He hadn't even mentioned the words 'Bible College' for nearly two years now, so how was she going to spring this upon him?

She had all day to think about it, and having given it some serious thought, came up with what she considered to be the best approach. Her plan was to wait until they were both in bed for the night, and either of them had switched out the light. It would be easier to tell him in the dark, she figured.

When Trevor came home that evening Esther acted normally but it was hard for her at times. She wondered, as she watched her husband busying about in ordinary routine matters, how he would react when she told him about her early morning encounter with God.

It was nearly eleven o'clock before all Esther's preconditions had been met. When they were in bed, with the light out, she whispered softly, "Trevor, I have something to tell you."

"What's that, love?" her husband replied, rather warily. Surely this couldn't be the opening of the next phase in the Esther House-extension Programme.

Trying to keep the weird mixture of trepidation and exhilaration that she felt in her fiercely pounding heart from manifesting itself in a tremble in her voice, Esther went on, "I believe God is calling me to go to Bible College."

The light flashed on again immediately.

Trevor jumped out of bed, and before his astonished wife could say another thing, he had dashed out the bedroom door. Esther imagined she heard him exclaim the one word, "Wonderful!" as he galloped down the stairs, but she couldn't be sure. She was dazzled by the sudden return of light to the bedroom and puzzled by Trevor's irrational reaction to her revelation.

Seconds later he came panting back into the bedroom.

He had the telephone directory tucked under one arm.

"What on earth are you doing with the telephone book?" Esther enquired, totally bewildered by all this baffling behaviour.

"I'm looking for the numbers of estate agents," came the matter-of-fact response, as though Esther should have known the next step after having confessed to being called of God. "We will be putting the house on the market in the morning."

The house on the market in the morning! The house that they had just spent so much time and money improving to their satisfaction, on the market! In the morning!

Yet Esther didn't object. She knew that if she was going to 'go' for God, her dream home would have to go to somebody else. That would be the way of it.

There was little sleeping, but a lot of excited talking and planning done, for the rest of that night. Trevor was praising God for answering his prayers. Esther was happy to submit to the will of God, and even more happy because Trevor was so happy.

They discussed many issues through 'the wee small hours.'

If they went to Bible College, would they have to pay? And if they did, where would the money come from, when Trevor gave up his job? What would they do about their involvement in the child-fostering programme? Would they be able to sell their furniture? What about the children's education?...

There were so many questions, but none of them were problems.

Trevor and Esther had always been taught that 'The Lord will provide', and though not sure how this would work in practice, for they had never put it to the test before, they were happy to leave it all to Him.

Next morning Trevor was in the estate agent's office shortly after opening time, and by lunchtime all the formalities had been completed, and their house was on the market.

Trevor and Esther were on their way to Bible College.

The only problem was that they knew precious little about Bible Colleges. They hadn't a clue where they were, who ran them, or what you had to do to get into them. With Esther not having 'felt ready to go' up until this moment Trevor had never even thought to enquire anything about them, having almost convinced himself that he would never see the inside of one.

Now, though, that they had both been called of God they decided that perhaps they had better suss out which one He would have them attend. Trevor and Esther did this in two ways. They began to pray very definitely for Divine guidance and they consulted a number of their more experienced Christian friends, many of whom were in The Faith Mission.

These friends advised the eager young couple to attend the Faith Mission Convention, which was taking place a few days later, over the Easter weekend. This annual convention is held in Bangor, Co. Down, and the Bible College meeting on Easter Sunday afternoon was recommended as being particularly suitable to Trevor and Esther

Although they had never been to Bangor in their lives before, Trevor and Esther set out to visit the seaside town that Sunday afternoon, accompanied by their close friend Garry. When they had located Hamilton Road Presbyterian Church where the rally was to be held, the three of them found seats downstairs on the left hand side, just below the gallery.

The pair of prospective Bible College students had their first comprehensive insight into college life all in the space of an hour and a half that Sunday afternoon. As a number of the current students stood up in groups to sing a selection of challenging Christian pieces, and as individuals to tell of their call to, and experiences in, Bible College, Trevor and Esther had their mind made up.

The Faith Mission Bible College in Edinburgh was the place for them.

They would apply as soon as they possibly could.

And the prospect of not being accepted never entered their head!

If God from heaven had called them to go, who on earth could stop them?

20

NINETY-NINE POINT NINE NINE PER CENT

"You should have a word with Bobby Dukelow," some of Trevor and Esther's friends who were well up in the ways and working of The Faith Mission advised them, when they began to enquire around about applying for Bible College. "Bobby's the Superintendent of the Irish Border District of the Mission. He lives in Portadown. Get in touch with him and he will keep you right."

Trevor was given Bobby's telephone number and rang him, as suggested. When Trevor had given him an outline of their conversion, and desire to attend Bible College as a preparation for entering some kind of Christian service, Bobby invited them to come for an interview.

A date and time were set. Bobby gave them directions to his home and they were to be there at 9.30 one morning. Esther acted as childminder to two pre-school children at that time, so on the morning of their interview appointment she brought Shauna, aged three, and David who was two, along with them in the car. She was sure it probably wouldn't take long, and one of them could stay out with the children while the other went in to talk to Mr. Dukelow. In any event they should be home later on that morning, well before the children's mothers arrived to collect them after work.

When they arrived outside the Faith Mission District Superintendent's house he came out to greet them. Trevor was just about to step out of the car, for they had decided on the way along that he would go in first. Then Bobby stooped down to speak in to both of them.

"You have come a fair bit already," he observed, cheerily. "We will go in my car."

Trevor and Esther looked at one another in consternation.

"Go where, Mr. Dukelow?" Trevor asked, when his powers of speech returned. "We thought the interview was here, with you."

"Oh no, no!" Bobby went on to explain what he had obviously either omitted to mention earlier or else assumed that the applicants already knew. "The interview isn't here. It's in Belfast. And it's not only with me. There will be a couple of the other main men from the Mission there as well, but you have nothing to worry about. They are very understanding."

Trevor looked over at Esther and her face had turned pale. Belfast! The only time she had ever been anywhere near Belfast in her life had been a few weeks earlier when they had passed through it going to Bangor. 'The North', as they called it in Monaghan was still in the throes of The Troubles at the time, and Esther had always imagined that people in Belfast were being shot in the head or bombed to bits at every other street corner.

Belfast! Why did they have to go to a perilous place that that?

There was no time to waste, however. Bobby seemed anxious to be off, and as soon as they had changed cars they set out.

As they sped down the motorway, Esther had the two children with her in the back seat, one on either side. Her nervousness about an interview had by then evaporated in a mist of anxiety about something else. The only thing she could think about was David and Shauna. Here they were, driving away from Monaghan, as hard as they could go. Would they ever be back home before their mothers called to collect them? And what would their parents say when they heard that she had taken them into such a 'dangerous' city?

On arriving in Belfast, Bobby escorted Trevor, Esther, and the two children round to The Faith Mission Bookshop, which was then in North Queen Street. When there the children quite enjoyed the adventure of weaving their way upstairs between all the boxes and piles of books of all kinds and colours, to the little tearoom on the second floor, where Trevor and Esther were to be interviewed.

When the two prospective candidates had found a seat their eyes met again. They were by this time almost numb with disbelief.

Esther was still concerned about the children. It was for a different reason, though, at that particular moment. What are these men going to think of us? she fretted. Imagine, turning up for what was patently a most important interview, with a three-year old and a two year-old, who weren't even your own, in tow!

Trevor, on the other hand, was more worried about whoever it was that was coming to see them. Just think of it, he mused. Here we are, a pair of spiritual novices, babes in the faith, 'country craiters' from Monaghan, waiting to be interviewed by some of the 'main men' of the Mission, spiritual giants, in Belfast. Wow! It was enough to make him want to grab hold of his wife and the two children and make a dash for freedom.

Then he thought of their dress. Esther and he had come for what they had imagined would be a cosy little chat with Bobby at his Portadown office, and had never even considered looking out their 'Sunday best' for the occasion. They were in their 'smart casual' attire. Would these men perhaps expect him to be in a suit, collar and tie?

Both of them had their fears allayed, at least to some extent, when the other two men who were to interview them entered the room. Willie Porter, who was Northern Ireland Superintendent of The Faith Mission at that time, and Edward Douglas, who ran the bookshop in which they were meeting, appeared more like warm and friendly father-figures than hard-hearted disciplinarians.

Bobby began by introducing them all to each other, and then inviting Trevor and Esther to tell what God had done in their lives, and why they would like to go to Bible College.

Trevor began by giving his testimony, up until the point where he was saved, then Esther took up the story, telling of what happened to her three days later. The young couple were greatly encouraged by the positive attitude and ongoing response of the 'interviewing panel' as they recounted the story of how God had used little Raymond's life and death to lead them to Him.

As they had been speaking Willie had been chiming in with a series of sonorous words or phrases throughout. He would put his head back, close his eyes, and with the light from the window glinting on his glasses utter a deep-throated 'Amen, 'Praise God,' or 'Praise the Lord.

When the stories were complete the three men appeared satisfied, and Edward remarked that it would be marvellous to hear that 'testimony double-act' from the pulpit. Trevor could start, leaving Esther to finish.

In the general conversation that followed in relation to the changes in lifestyle that a spell in Bible College would bring about for a married couple with a young family, Edward Douglas quoted words which Trevor and Esther had never heard before. They remembered them immediately, however, and that quotation was to prove a source of strength and encouragement to them in difficult days to come.

The words were, 'If Jesus Christ be God, and died for me, then there is no sacrifice too great for me to make for Him.'

With the interviews over the three men told Trevor and Esther that they would tell them of their decision later, and that they had one or two other items of business to discuss. The young couple then turned their attention back to Shauna and David who had been very well-behaved throughout, as there was so much to investigate around the little room to which they had been restricted for nearly an hour.

While 'the main men from the Mission' continued their deliberations, Trevor and Esther arrived out on the streets of Belfast with two hungry little kids by the hand. On making enquiries about somewhere to 'get a bite to eat' they learnt that there was 'a restaurant called The Skandia' just around the corner in Howard Street.

The four of them had their lunch in 'The Skandia' and when they were finished Bobby was ready to head back towards Portadown.

As they were racing back up the M1 towards County Armagh Trevor could curb his curiosity no longer. The interviewers had told the eager young couple that they would inform them of their decision 'later.' This was 'later,' but they still hadn't heard anything.

Leaning across to Bobby, so that he would hear him over the whine of the engine, Trevor ventured to ask, "Do you think we will be going to Bible College O.K., Bobby?"

Bobby smiled knowingly before replying, "I am ninety-nine point nine nine per cent sure that the pair of you will be going all right, Trevor."

Before Trevor and Esther left Bobby's car in Portadown, to continue their journey to Monaghan, Bobby handed Trevor a brown envelope. "Those are the application forms for the Bible College, Trevor," he told him. "Could you and Esther fill them in and send them back to me within two weeks?"

They promised they would and set out for home. There was so much to discuss on the way, and Esther was thankful that she was going to make it to Monaghan before David and Shauna's parents were due to collect them.

Everything had worked out well in the end.

All that remained for them to do now was complete the application forms for Bible College.

That, however, was to prove easier said than done.

The brown envelope was laid carefully aside for a while after they arrived home for there were so many other things to see to. It was bedtime before Trevor and Esther were both free to look at the forms together. Sitting up in bed they read them over with a view to completing them and then sending them off the next morning.

It was then that they realised they had a problem.

Some of the questions were plain enough, and easily answered. For example there was one inviting the applicant to give details of his or her level of educational attainment.

Esther had completed her Junior Certificate and was able to list the grades achieved. Trevor, on the other hand, had opted out of school to start work at the earliest possible opportunity, without even bothering to sit any final examinations. His 'level of educational achievement' was easily described. It could be summed up in a single word.

He simply wrote, 'NONE.'

Some of the other questions, though, were not quite so straightforward for Trevor and Esther. They were couched in theological terms, and alluded to doctrinal matters, none of which they had a clue about. Even if someone had been available to translate them into language they could understand it would still have been doubtful if they could have identified, not to mention give a reasoned response to, the issues involved.

They discussed these questions at length, trying to figure out what they meant, before writing down what they considered to be relevant answers. Then they decided, on reflection, that their responses could have been better expressed. So they changed them. And then they changed them again.

After almost an hour spent deliberating on how they should respond to various questions, and having made three of four attempts at some of them, Trevor and Esther were frazzled and the forms were an absolute mess.

"This is hopeless, Trevor!" Esther exclaimed at last. "Now that we are satisfied about what we ought to be putting on the forms, we can't send them in. Look at them! They are like a dog's dinner! We will have to get a new set of forms. I will phone Bobby in the morning."

With that she screwed the fouled up forms into tiny balls of crumpled paper and tossed them across the bedroom towards the little bin in the corner.

Esther did as she had intimated, and rang Bobby after returning from leaving the children to school the following morning. She explained that they would like a new set of forms because they 'hadn't been very sure about some of the answers' and so had 'made a bit of a mess' of the originals.

"No problem," Bobby replied "I'll post them off to you as soon as I can. They will be with you in the next day or two."

He kept his promise and two days later Trevor and Esther had a new set of forms and were in a position to start all over again. It wasn't quite so hard second time round for they now knew what they wanted to say in reply to most of the questions.

There was one question, though, that hadn't presented them with the slightest difficulty at either their first or second attempt, neither with making a definite decision nor knowing how to express it.

It was one of the last on the application form, and asked, 'Do you intend to stay in the work of The Faith Mission after training?'

Trevor and Esther had already made up their minds that when they had completed their course they would like to go out as missionary house-parents to somewhere in Africa. Thus when it came to answering this question they were wholeheartedly agreed that their joint response could be most simply conveyed in a single word.

It was 'NO.'

They never at any time thought to take into account that such an answer could have a negative effect on their possible acceptance to college. God had called them to go and that was it. To them filling up forms was nothing more than a fiddling frustrating formality.

With their applications eventually completed to their satisfaction they posted them off and continued to prepare to go to Bible College, before receiving any official confirmation of their acceptance.

It seemed that they had no sooner sent away their forms than the interest in buying their house increased. A number of prospective purchasers began bidding for it. A few of them dropped out of the race early on leaving only two very keen would-be buyers to bid against one another. This went on for days, and by the time Trevor and Esther's house was sold they had received far more for it than they had ever expected.

Shortly after the sale of their house had been confirmed Trevor and Esther were officially notified that they had been accepted for a two-year course at The Faith Mission Bible College in Edinburgh, beginning in late September. They felt so thrilled that God had led them, and provided for them, 'beyond all that they could ask or think,' so far. All that remained for them to do now was make their final preparations for going.

They contacted the college and arranged to go there six weeks before the start of the course so that Darren and Gregory could both commence their new school at the beginning of the autumn term in the last week of August.

Trevor and Esther had a house to clear before a completion date in early July and so they gave away all of their furniture except beds for the boys and them to sleep in, and a wardrobe in which to keep what few clothes they needed. They then moved those few essential items of furniture into a room Garry very kindly offered to let them have in his house, and that is where they stayed until it was time to leave for Edinburgh.

All their kitchen utensils and cutlery had also been donated to anyone who could make use of them. They had kept only four each of knives, forks, spoons, cups and plates, and a couple of saucepans.

When the big morning came to leave for the ferry to cross to Scotland, all Trevor and Esther had retained to bring with them for Darren, Gregory and themselves fitted easily into the boot of their Toyota Carina Mark II.

It was all so exciting. So thrilling. They felt that they were setting out as a family on a big adventure with God.

Driving northeastwards from Stranraer towards Edinburgh they felt that they were at least three of four rungs up Jacob's ladder.

They were, they thought, halfway to heaven.

21

THE FIFTY-POUND NOTE

When Trevor and Esther arrived at the Faith Mission College in mid-August there were very few people around. Lectures weren't due to begin for another six weeks, but the new students could barely wait to get started doing something for, or learning more about, God.

It was still the middle of the summer vacation and some of the college buildings were being repainted. With the redecorating of his house in progress the Assistant Principal and his family had been given temporary accommodation in the flat which had been allocated to Trevor and Esther in 'the married quarters.' This in turn meant that their first few weeks in Bible College were to be spent living all day in the Student Common Room, and sleeping on mattresses spread out on the floor of it at night.

Although this wasn't exactly their idea of heaven, Trevor and Esther were so delighted to be even on the Bible College campus that the Common Room floor still felt like hallowed ground to them. They didn't mind it at all.

They were happy, too, to be able to make some preparations for embarking on their study course, which would begin later in the term. Dr. Colin Peckham, the College Principal, had given them the titles of their assignments to allow them to engage in some preparatory reading. He also furnished them with a list of the memory verses which they were expected to have learnt by Christmas.

These activities gave Trevor and Esther something to focus on after the Primary School term recommenced. With the boys now both in full-time education they had a few free hours in the middle of the day.

Trevor found settling down to study a lot more of a trial than his wife did. She had been at least interested in school in her teenage years. He hadn't. He had hated it. Trevor had never studied anything of an academic nature seriously in his life and all of a sudden he was being expected to read reams of stuff and learn chunks of the Bible off by heart!

The learning of the verses was a real problem to him at first. He found it very disheartening when he couldn't get them to stick in his head and his exasperation was exacerbated a hundredfold when he watched Esther learning hers. It seemed that all she had to do was read any verse over three or four times and she knew it while it was taking him the most of a week to learn it!

And Dr. Peckham had told them in one of their first meetings that they would be expected to have learnt 260 important scripture texts over their two years in Edinburgh.

Could *that* be heaven on earth for Trevor?

It wasn't, initially, but he was later to discover that the mental discipline required to persist in the learning of a memory verse was to help him as he undertook more detailed study.

The Faith Mission Convention in Edinburgh was held in late August and Trevor and Esther went along as often as possible. They thought it great to hear a different range of speakers and Esther was challenged about her personal suitability for the work of the Lord at one of the sessions.

The theme of the speaker's talk that evening was 'laying all on the altar for God.' He pointed out that to be effective in Christian work the servant of the Lord should be living a cleansed life, totally surrendered to his Master. He invited his audience, on a number of occasions, to 'examine their own lives,' to make sure that they were not harbouring any sins, or even attitudes, that could be a hindrance to the work or a stumbling block to others.

Esther immediately thought of her fierce temper. There were times, even since conversion, when she had 'flown off the handle,' with only minimal provocation. This had been worrying her, and she was forced to recognise in the meeting that she needed the help of the Lord in dealing with it.

At the end of his address the speaker invited anyone who wanted to hand over their lives completely to the Lord 'to come forward during the singing of the last hymn.'

This was a hymn which he had specially chosen to bring his message of the evening to a fitting conclusion.

It began, 'Lord, I make a full surrender,
All I have I yield to Thee,
For Thy love so great and tender,
Asks a gift from me.

During the singing of the fourth verse Esther stepped out and made her way up to the front of the hall. The words being sung around her expressed exactly the sentiments of her heart.

They were, 'Lord, I lay my life before Thee,
Hear, this hour, this sacred vow,
All Thine own I now restore Thee,
Thine for ever now.'

Having remained at the front until the hymn was finished Esther was then shown into a small side room where a worker talked to her and prayed with her.

When Esther returned to her room that evening she was certain that God had given her a new sense of tranquillity in her life and that He would help her to overcome those violent, and often unprovoked, outbursts of temper. That conviction would no doubt be put to the test during the days and weeks to come.

A few days later Esther had taken the two boys to one of the Children's Meetings in the convention and after they came home little Gregory said, "Mummy, I would like to give my life to Jesus."

His mummy was overjoyed at this simple declaration and sat down beside him at once. She told him of the Saviour who loved little children and called them to come to Him and Gregory accepted Jesus into his heart, sitting by her side.

Esther felt this to be a crowning blessing on her earlier commitment. She had now led two people to faith in Jesus Christ. And they were her own two children.

When the college activities got into full swing in late September Trevor and Esther threw themselves into their studies with a will. Trevor found it particularly difficult to settle down to systematic study, but he loved his Bible and he loved the Lord so he carried on and gradually became more accustomed to it. Esther enjoyed her studies from the start but as the year progressed she was to find her Christian patience, and commitment to 'exclusively peaceful means,' tried to the utmost.

One day she overheard something that she chose to ignore, trying to believe that she hadn't heard it at all. Surely it could only be a figment of her imagination. It wasn't, though. For she was soon to hear it again. And then again. What she had heard being done behind her back was now being practised well within earshot.

Many of the students, and the children of some of the married couples, had begun to mimic Esther's heavy Cavan brogue quite mercilessly. Although this was done under the pretence of being funny, Esther got the impression that those who were mocking her accent were actually laughing at her, and not with her. She found it more offensive than funny, more hurtful than hilarious. What cut her to the quick in her simple, honest faith, was that the people who were doing this to her were actually Christians, who were supposed to be loving and caring for one another, if she understood her Bible correctly. And what was to her even more incredulous was that these people were actually at *Bible College* training for full-time Christian service.

Was this really heaven for her?

By the middle of their second term in Edinburgh Esther was doing well in all her college work but had been smitten with an inferiority complex because of her accent. As the taunting continued unchecked she began to feel inhibited every time she opened her mouth in public.

The former, fierce Esther would have lost her temper and turned on her mockers. The now miraculously more controlled Esther didn't, however. Instead she mentioned it to Dr. Peckham one day when she was talking over a number of issues related to her college course with him. She explained how she had begun to feel so self-conscious about speaking to others both in meetings and on the campus because of how her strong southern Irish accent was being constantly aped.

"Don't worry about that, Esther," her Principal advised. "Everybody here has an accent except you." That was the positive way to look at it, and Esther certainly found it a lot easier to cope from then on.

Despite a number of minor difficulties and disappointments Trevor and Esther enjoyed their first year at Bible College and were constantly amazed at how God supplied all their needs.

When they arrived back in Edinburgh after the Christmas break they paid some bills that were due in relation to their course in the new term, and made provision for feeding the four of them. They called the matters that always required attention at the commencement of any new term the three 'F's.' Fees, food and fare. They stocked their kitchen with food, paid their fees and booked and paid for their ferry trip back home for the next vacation.

Having settled all these matters in January 1990, Esther found that she had nothing left in her purse but one fifty-pound note. That was all they had to keep them in clothes, put petrol in the car and buy any extras either they or the children might need in the foreseeable future. It was going to be tight, she reckoned.

All her housekeeping plans were thrown into complete disarray on just their second Saturday morning back. Trevor came up to the flat and said, "Esther we need two new tyres on the car. I have been down at her there. Two of the tyres are flat and are not worth repairing. They are nearly bald. I need fifty pounds to get a couple of new ones."

"Fifty pounds!" Esther exclaimed. "You probably don't realise it but that is all I have in my purse at the minute to keep us for the rest of the term. Fifty pounds. Can you not get them any cheaper than that?"

"No I can't, Esther," her husband replied. "I said fifty-pounds but it's actually forty-eight pounds fifty. I didn't think there was all that much of a difference. And that's for a pair of remoulds. I have been phoning around all the tyre places. We need them, Esther. Otherwise we are never going to be going anywhere".

"Well, I'm sorry, Trevor, but you are not getting my last fifty pounds," Esther insisted.

"Please, Esther," Trevor begged. "We need them. If you give me that money I'm quite sure the Lord will provide for us. He knows our needs."

"Yes Trevor, I know that. And we have experienced that before. But this is different. How can I hand over all the money we have to put tyres on a car? And be left to face the weekend with absolutely nothing!" his wife countered.

The tension was too much for her. She had started to cry.

Trevor persisted, and when he had assured her repeatedly that the Lord would provide, although secretly he didn't know how, Esther tearfully handed over their last fifty pounds.

They spent the weekend as Esther had predicted they would, without a penny in their purse, but on Monday something miraculous happened. Just as Trevor had predicted it would.

In the afternoon Trevor and Esther agreed to give Gail, one of the other college students, a lift into Edinburgh city centre in the car, and when they were waiting for her to come out and join them, Esther remarked, "You know Trevor, this is crazy. We are using the last petrol we have in our tank to drive into the city centre where we wont be able to buy anything for we have no money."

"Don't worry, Esther. The Lord will provide," came the reply.

Trevor had just begun to wonder if he had been right to keep telling his wife that. He couldn't stop now though. It was important to keep up her confidence.

Esther rolled her eyes at him, sighed, said nothing, and looked away. She didn't want him to see any more tears. There could be no more conversation anyway for Gail had just come alongside and was opening the door of the car.

When they were almost into the city centre the student in the back leaned forward between the two front seats. She then reached over a hand towards Esther.

"I would like you to take this from me," she said, softly. "It is my tithe, and ever since Trevor offered to give me a lift God has been telling me to give it to you. I don't know why, but here it is. Please, Esther, could you take it?"

Esther reached up her hand to receive whatever it was that the girl wanted to give her and discovered, to her astonishment, that it was a neatly folded fifty pound note.

Gail had never heard the tale of the tyres and yet God had told her to give Trevor and Esther her tithe!

The Lord had provided for them, in spite of their doubts and fears. Nor did He leave it there. It was to be ongoing for the remainder of the term. From that January afternoon, until they set off to return to Ireland for their Easter break, Esther had never any less than fifty pounds in her purse.

Each new term seemed to bring with it a new test of their faith, however.

In late May the college arranged an outing for all their staff and students plus their families. It promised to be a great day out, but Trevor and Esther had a problem. They had no money left. They were back to the tyres on the car scenario. Expenses, which they had no visible means of meeting, were raising their ugly heads once more.

The boys were so looking forward to the outing with all the other children, but how could Trevor and Esther take them? They didn't even have enough money to buy them an ice cream!

First thing in the morning, on the day of the outing, Trevor drove down to the bank to check their account at the 'hole-in-the-wall.' There was nothing in it.

By the time he returned to the college campus he was wondering what kind of an excuse they could make for not going on the outing.

The post had arrived when he was away, however, and there were two letters addressed to Mr.& Mrs. Trevor Gillanders. He picked these up and went in search of his wife.

It was a lovely late spring morning and Esther was sitting out on the veranda, supposedly learning memory verses, but actually chatting away to Sharon, the college cook. Trevor and Esther had become very friendly with Sharon, who had looked after the boys for them on a number of occasions earlier in the year when they had been studying for exams.

In the course of conversation Esther had told her that Trevor had gone down to see if they had anything left in their account. When they were discussing the subject of money Sharon shared with Esther that she was also 'broke,' and didn't know what she was going to do about the outing.

When Trevor eventually located them he said to Esther, "There's nothing in the bank, but there are a couple of letters here for us."

"Is there anything down there for me?" Sharon asked, with an undisguised eagerness.

"No, Sharon. Well at least I didn't notice anything," Trevor told her gently, gathering that she was possibly hoping for something.

When Trevor opened the first envelope he found that it was from Mrs. Elizabeth Dudgeon in Moira, Northern Ireland. Trevor read out the accompanying short note. It said,

'Dear Trevor and Esther,

The Lord has laid it on my heart that you have a need and I feel that I have to do something about it. I trust that the little gift enclosed in this letter will help meet that need, whatever it is…'

Her 'little gift' was twenty pounds.

The other letter had a Canadian stamp on it, and when Trevor slit it open he found that it was from Ken and Louise Clipsham. They were a couple who were working with the Faith Mission in Canada and had also felt 'led' to send a gift to Trevor and Esther. It turned out to be a cheque for forty Canadian dollars.

As Trevor and Esther began to praise God for His provision for them Sharon suddenly burst into tears.

"Why is it," she said through her sobs, "that God has provided for you and He hasn't provided for me?"

Esther was quick to chip in. "Hold on a minute, Sharon," she told her. "Don't say that. When God provided for us He provided for you too. It's not by chance that you were here when we opened those letters. There's enough here to meet the need of all of us. We will share this with you."

When Trevor and Esther were preparing for their day out, back in their flat an hour or so later, Trevor said, "You know, Esther, I never cease to be amazed at the Lord's provision. It took that letter two days to come. God had told Elizabeth about our need before we even knew we had it!"

22

CLOSE ENCOUNTERS OF DIFFERENT KINDS

On the day after leaving Edinburgh at the end of their first year in Bible College Trevor and Esther embarked upon a four-week period of summer work. This was a compulsory constituent of the Faith Mission training programme. Married couples with families were expected to spend four weeks in a practical situation over the summer, as they had to return to the Scottish capital in August to see their children safely back to school. Most other students were required to complete eight weeks service before returning to college at the end of September.

Trevor and Esther had been assigned to the south Irish district, and specifically to the campsite in Bandon, County Cork, for their first experience of Mission life..

The couple were tired as they set out in the morning having just completed a set of examinations that week and then packed up and travelled across from Edinburgh to Monaghan the previous day. They realised that it would be a six or seven-hour journey south to Cork and the children would no doubt find it tedious. Trevor was determined to make as good time as possible, though, for he had a reason to keep him upbeat, despite the long drive.

It was Saturday, June 30, and Italia 90, the World Cup football competition, was reaching its climax. Ireland was scheduled to play the host nation, Italy, in the quarter-finals that evening. The entire match was to be broadcast live and he thought it would be great to be at their destination and well settled in before it came on, so that he could watch it. That would be one way of unwinding after a wearisome week, and before beginning his work schedule the next day.

Having eventually arrived, tired but full of anticipation of an evening spent relaxing with his family in front of the television before beginning the next day to teach the scriptures to some eager young people, Trevor had 'the wind fairly taken out of his sails.'

He had just stepped out of the car, and Esther and the two boys were all still in it when the resident leader came out and said to him, by way of a welcome, "There are some broken windows around the campsite that we need fixed as soon as possible. I would like you to get started putting glass into them immediately."

Thus began Trevor and Esther's first term of service with The Faith Mission. Trevor became a glazier for the evening, and Esther settled the boys and herself into their accommodation. It was ten thirty before darkness fell and Trevor could work no more. By that time the match he had so much looked forward to watching was long since over, he hadn't seen a ball kicked and he was absolutely exhausted.

During the first week there Trevor and Esther were allocated their separate roles in the running of the camp. Trevor was responsible for looking after all the needs of the boys attending it, and this meant that he was effectively on duty twenty-four hours a day. He was also a dormitory leader and slept in the same room as eleven of the boys every night. During the day his two sons were able to enjoy the programme of activities under their dad's supervision. The weather was lovely and it wasn't long before Trevor and his two sons were sporting healthy suntans.

There was little chance of Esther enjoying much of the sunshine, however. She was disappointed to discover that she was expected to serve as a full-time kitchen maid. After a year of study at Bible College she was dismayed to find that her first engagement for the Lord was to consist of helping to prepare and serve meals, keep worktops tidy, brush floors and take her turn at cleaning the toilets.

Her only opportunity to reach out to others with the Christian message over the entire four week period was during one of the weeks when she was allocated a fifteen-minute slot each evening to tell a missionary story, and on a single occasion when she was asked to speak during an open air service.

She often lay awake at nights wondering what she was doing there. When God had called her to dedicate her life to His service, her excuse of 'making the tea' had sounded so pitiful. Now here she was doing that very thing She found it somewhat confusing.

After his initial disappointment, Trevor was, by contrast, beginning to enjoy life, and the blessing of the Lord, as the camp weeks followed one after another. He found it rewarding to work with the boys during the day and was thrilled to have been used to point some of the lads in his dormitory to faith in Christ during the evening 'quiet times.'

This disparity of experience was most evident on the rare occasions when Trevor and Esther met each other on the site, often when Esther was hurrying either to or from one or other of her chores, during those very busy days. Married life for the couple had been put on hold and they had become like 'ships passing in the night.'

During such fleeting encounters, the pale faced-wife would raise both arms in a gesture of dejection as she approached her bronzed husband. As they came face to face she would then place a finger up to her lips. Those two signs, coming in quick succession, were calculated to say, in effect, 'Pease don't speak to me, Trevor. I am liable to burst into tears at any minute!'

Towards the end of their four-week term an outing had been arranged for all the camp workers. It was to a ten-pin bowling alley in Cork. Trevor went along to the outing, but Esther opted to remain back at camp so that she could put the boys to bed early for 'a good night's sleep. Since it was a Friday night and there were no campers on site she could allow them to sleep in a dormitory across the way from the room she shared with them. This had the dual benefit of allowing them to sleep undisturbed and it meant she didn't have to tiptoe about to avoid wakening them.

As Trevor was entering the bowling alley he passed an amusement arcade. He looked in and saw dozens of teenagers milling about. Many of them were standing feeding money into the fruit machines, 'the one-arm bandits.' He stopped and watched them for a moment, and then said inwardly, "Lord, who is reaching out to these young people?" He thought initially that he was addressing the Lord, but it was actually God who was speaking to him.

It was as though He were saying, 'Forget about Africa, Trevor. What about Ireland? If you don't do something about your own country, who will?'

A seed had been sown in his mind. Would it bear fruit, though? A spark had been ignited. But would it start a fire in his soul?

Meanwhile, back on the campsite, a close encounter of a very different kind was taking place.

Esther had been glad to enjoy a break from the hectic round of activity, and afforded herself the luxury of a prolonged period of prayer and Bible reading before going to bed.

She hadn't turned the light out very long, however, until she felt an inexplicable, but tangible, presence of evil in the room. Within minutes she had stiffened and was soon lying like a terrified stick in the bed. Her strength had gone. She wanted to reach out and put on the light, but something held her back.

It was the thought of the memory verse she had been teaching the children during her missionary story. It was, 'God is light, and in Him is no darkness at all.' She had been teaching them that if we relied on God, who is light, then the powers of darkness and evil couldn't harm us. God seemed to rebuke her with this recollection, saying that if she resorted to putting on the light she would be defeating all that she had been trying to instil into the young people. Was she actually telling children they could trust in God to help them defeat the powers of evil in their lives, and yet she wasn't prepared to trust Him herself?

All Esther could do was pray. She pleaded with God fervently, and repeatedly, to protect her. She was soon lying with the bedclothes pulled right up to her neck, afraid even to put her hands out for if she did she was sure she would have touched the Devil. The spectre of evil was all around her, and frighteningly close. And still Esther cried out to God in her soul, ceaselessly and desperately.

After more than an hour in the grip of genuine terror, encompassed, but unharmed, by demonic power, Esther saw the headlights of the cars returning from the night out, flash on to the bedroom window. Trevor and the others were back and within minutes Esther began to relax. The presence had withdrawn from the room.

It had been a spine-chilling and unforgettable confrontation.

At the end of the four weeks Trevor had fallen in love with the work of the Lord. He had been fully involved in all the activities of the camp, and felt that any little he had been able to do had been approved of God.

Esther, however, had been left with a totally different impression. She ended up mentally confused, physically exhausted, emotionally drained and spiritually flat. On the Saturday they left she cried, from both wretchedness and relief, all the way back from Cork to Monaghan, a journey of just over six hours.

Having had a short holiday after their contrasting summer work experiences Trevor and Esther returned to Edinburgh in mid-August before the start of another school and college term.

Before Christmas of that, their second and final year at the Bible College, they both felt that what God was calling them to do was the very thing that they hadn't, initially, wanted to do. They thought back to their emphatic 'NO' on the college application form, but recognised that God had plans for them, which they didn't have for themselves. A number of factors, including Trevor's having been challenged in Cork about the spiritual needs of 'the young people of Ireland,' led them to change their minds and apply for full-time service with The Faith Mission.

In addition to a busy round of studying and fulfilling preaching engagements during their last two terms at Bible College, Trevor and Esther continued to pray that God would show them His will for their lives. They assumed that He had done so when, just before they graduated, they received confirmation that their application had been successful.

On graduating, Trevor and Esther were informed of their engagements for the next year as full-time workers with The Faith Mission.

Their first meeting was to be in a tent mission, conducted by Trevor Matthews and Rev. William Smylie in Desertmartin, County Londonderry. There they were each to tell of their conversion and call into Christian service in preparation for their first one-year posting. That was to be in the nearby town of Magherafelt, commencing in September.

Having told of what God had done for them, and what they prayed that He would do through them, in Desertmartin, Trevor and Esther set off to fulfil their second summer assignment.

This was to work on a campsite in Stradbally, in the midlands of Ireland. When Esther learnt of this commission her spontaneous reaction was, "Oh no! That will probably just mean another kitchen for me!"

It wasn't at all like that, however. Although both Trevor and Esther had to assist with the daily chores of the camp, Esther was much happier for a number of reasons. To start with, one of the local Christians, Edward Moynan, had given them the use of a house in which they could live as a family for the summer, in nearby Durrow. This, plus the fact that she was able to become actively involved in the outdoor Children's Clubs in Portlaoise, and conduct Bible studies and 'quiet times' with the campers, helped encourage her as a servant of the Lord.

The couple were extremely happy in Durrow but they both wakened with a strangely uneasy feeling one Sunday morning when there. As they were preparing breakfast Esther said, "I had a very restless night, last night. I dreamt that mummy had cancer. It was so real it was scary."

Trevor stopped what he was doing and looked across at her. "Is that right, Esther?" he began, appearing startled. "It's funny for I had a dream, too, only I dreamt that it was my mum who had cancer."

It sounded too sinister to be ignored so Trevor and Esther forgot about breakfast in the meantime, found the two boys, and all four of them headed out to the car. The children were surprised to be driving down through the deserted streets of Durrow and didn't for the moment know where their parents were taking them.

All was soon to be revealed. Trevor and Esther remembered that there were two telephone boxes side by side in the town centre and that was their destination. On reaching them husband and wife took one each. They would never rest, they reckoned, until they had checked that their mums were O.K.

After the clink of coins in machines a couple of conversations commenced. Esther was the first to react. She hadn't been long on the phone before she knocked the window dividing her from her husband, and gave him a thumbs-up sign.

She didn't get one back, though.

Trevor was engaged in very earnest dialogue with someone at the other end of the line. It was his sister-in-law.

When Trevor phoned her she said at once, "I'm glad to hear you, Trevor. We were trying to contact you yesterday, but couldn't. I'm afraid we have a bit of bad news. Your mum has just been diagnosed with breast cancer."

It was a shock, and although the family was understandably worried about their mother's state of health Trevor had an additional concern. He was also anxious about her spiritual welfare.

With the summer work completed, one of Trevor and Esther's first calls when they returned to Monaghan was with his mum. They hadn't been talking long until Trevor had all his fears allayed when his mum told him of what had happened to her a few months earlier.

She had, she said, been listening to her granddaughter Nicola reading Psalm 51 from the Bible. Near the beginning of the psalm she had read the words, 'Wash me thoroughly from my iniquity, and cleanse me from my sin.' Shortly after that, the desire of the psalmist seemed to be repeated with the request, 'Purge me with hyssop, and I shall be clean. Wash me and I shall by whiter that snow.'

Trevor was thrilled to hear his mother confess that when she had sat and listened to the words 'Wash me and I shall be whiter than snow,' she had just said in her heart, "Lord, please do that for me."

What a consolation to Trevor, what an answer to prayer!

In late August, Trevor and Esther moved into a new bungalow in Magherafelt so that they would be in a position to start their work in September. Robert Ferguson, a Christian from the area, had built the bungalow, but wasn't ready to live in it, and so was happy for Trevor and Esther to use it during their planned year in the town.

When Trevor Matthews, the District Superintendent of the Mission, called to see them one day as they were settling in, he handed Esther a scrap of paper. There was a telephone number on it.

"Some woman passed that on to me on the way out of the tent mission in Desertmartin, the night Trevor and you gave your testimonies," he explained. "She said that her husband and she would like you to give them a ring when you came to live in Magherafelt."

Who could they be? the new resident workers in the County Londonderry town were left to wonder. And why did they want Trevor and Esther to contact them?

23

THE LOVELY COUPLE

Trevor and Esther soon settled into their new home in Magherafelt
and Darren and Gregory were enrolled in local schools at the
beginning of September 1991.

Towards the middle of that month Trevor remarked to his wife
one day, "What should we do about that phone number Trevor
Matthews passed on to us after the meeting in Desertmartin, Esther?
It is a sort of awkward trying to phone somebody up when you don't
even know their name!"

Since they were living in a recently completed bungalow, and
were still waiting for the telephone to be installed, Esther suggested
that the next time he was in Magherafelt he should 'give them a ring
from a phone box.'

It was Friday morning before he was in the town again and when
there Trevor called the number on the slip of paper.

A woman's voice answered and Trevor explained that he was

ringing because someone had requested that he should do so, after a testimony meeting during a tent mission in Desertmartin during the summer.

"Oh yes. You don't know us, but I'm Ruth Moffett and my husband is called Jim," the lady replied, sounding pleased. "We are from Magherafelt and when we heard that you were coming to live in the town the Lord seemed to impress upon our hearts to make contact with you."

Trevor had just begun to thank Ruth very much for her interest when she went on, "Where are you living? I'm free this morning and I would like to call out and meet you and your wife."

When he had given Ruth precise directions to the bungalow, which was on a main road about two miles out of Magherafelt, Trevor went back home and told Esther about the woman who had asked to come out and see them. She had, he reported, 'sounded very friendly on the phone.'

An hour later a red Vauxhall Cavalier came up the drive and stopped outside Trevor and Esther's new home. It was the lady Trevor had phoned, making her introductory visit.

"Don't close the door yet," she said to Esther, as they were standing chatting out at the front. "I have something for you and if you don't mind I might as well bring it in now."

What she had for them was a huge box of groceries. As Esther looked at it she realised that it contained everything she would need to keep all four of them for a long time to come. Both Trevor and she thanked Ruth profusely, for what the kind lady didn't know, nor did they tell her at the time, was that they had only seven pounds left between them. They had been discussing earlier how best to spend it to see them 'over the weekend.'

Ruth didn't stay long but as she was leaving she said, "I must go now, but I will come back soon and bring Jim along with me to meet you. If there's anything you need in the meantime, though, please don't hesitate to let us know."

That afternoon Ruth met Kathleen Ritchie, another Christian lady whom she knew, in Magherafelt. She told Kathleen that she had just been out that morning to meet the new Faith Mission couple who had come to work in the district. "You ought to go out and see them sometime," she advocated. "I'm sure they would appreciate a call."

Trevor was surprised to see a second strange car turn into their drive in the same day when Kathleen took Ruth up on her suggestion later that afternoon. He was sitting in a large chair in the bay window when she arrived, for he had a very sore back. For more than a week he had been shovelling, wheeling and then spreading gravel stones to make a drive up to and around their home. Lorries had tipped them out by the ton and he had undertaken to do the rest. All the hard work had exacerbated an old back injury and at that moment he was in agony.

"Are you Mrs. Gillanders?" the stranger at the door enquired after Esther had opened it to her.

" Yes, I am." Esther was somewhat hesitant in her reply for she hadn't been expecting anybody else that day.

"Pleased to meet you," the visitor continued cheerily. "I'm Kathleen Ritchie. I met Ruth in the town earlier on and she was telling me you had come to live in the area."

Esther invited her in and they talked for a short time before Kathleen said, "I'm sorry but I'll have to go again. It's nearly teatime and my husband Wray will soon be home. But if you don't mind he and I will both call out to see you again some of these days."

She then left and soon after her husband had arrived home for the tea she had gone in to make him, she said, "I have just been out to meet the new Faith Mission workers in the area, Wray. They are a lovely couple. I promised them that we would be out again sometime."

They were the first to keep their promise to return, and when they did so, early on Sunday afternoon, Darren was lying on a settee all wrapped up in a rug. He had always been troubled with asthma and living in a drying out house had aggravated his condition.

As they were sitting around in the living room, Wray, who was becoming really concerned for the health of the asthmatic child whom he had just recently met, commented, "Esther, I hope you don't mind me saying but would you not consider putting something more on that fire? Do you not think the house is very cold?"

"No I don't think so, Wray," was Esther's answer. "We are tough you know." She tried to pass it off as a joke. But it was no joke.

The truth was that the house **was** indeed cold. Her feet were like blocks of ice and her fingertips were numb. Yet what she couldn't tell Wray was that they had an open fire and an oil-fired boiler, either or both of which could be used to provide them with central heating, but they couldn't afford the fuel. Trevor and she had decided to keep their seven pounds to put petrol in the car and so she had spent the previous afternoon collecting what firewood she could from the hedges round about.

What Wray didn't realize was that if he stayed much longer the house was set to become even colder, for the few green sticks that were fizzing in the grate were all that remained of the intrepid mother's Saturday afternoon wood gathering.

Esther was embarrassed but slightly relieved when Kathleen and Wray soon excused themselves and left. Trevor and she were both disappointed that the air in their house hadn't been as warm as the feeling in their hearts for them when they called.

There was nothing else, though, that Esther could have done or said in the circumstances. She was definitely not going to reveal their poverty-stricken state. As Faith Mission workers they were depending on God to supply all their need. He had used Ruth to provide them with enough food to do for a long time.

What could He do about fuel, though? Their situation was desperate.

Less than an hour after Wray and Kathleen had left Esther spotted a small pick-up truck out on the road with its flashers indicating that it was about to turn into their drive.

"Who can this be coming now, Trevor?" she said, beckoning to her husband to come across and join her at the window.

"It must be Robert," Trevor responded. "He's the only one I can think of who might have a truck like that. I wonder what he wants. It would be odd for him to come on a Sunday, though."

Their idea that perhaps it was the owner of the bungalow come to call about something was reinforced when the truck drove on round to the back rather than pulling up at the front as most people did.

On opening the back door they were to discover that it wasn't

Robert, but Wray back with his son-in-law Noel. "We've something for you here," Wray said, and without stopping for any further chit-chat began helping Noel unload bags of coal and blocks from the back of the truck.

When they had finished Wray explained how they were able to get their hands on so much fuel so quickly. "These are the sticks and coal we had lying out in our back yard after we changed our heating system," he told the amazed, but extremely grateful Trevor and Esther. "We felt that you could probably make use of them."

What he didn't go on to say, however, was that Kathleen had been pestering him for months to 'clear all that coal and stuff out of the back yard.' His reply to her repeated requests had always been, "Don't worry. I'll do it when I find somebody that needs it."

Now he believed God had led them to those needy people. He had never envisaged, however, when he was making his excuses to Kathleen, that he would end up changing out of his 'good clothes' to clear out the yard on a Sunday afternoon!

Noel and he hadn't long driven away from the back of the bungalow until Esther had a big fire roaring up the chimney and the radiators in every room soon began to tick and click with the hot water passing through them.

Trevor, however, didn't have time to enjoy the first real heat they had experienced in the house for days. He soon had to leave to go and speak in a meeting in Ballygelly, near Broughshane in County Antrim. This was in preparation for a mission which he and two other workers were scheduled to commence the following Sunday.

Soon after he left, Darren's condition began to deteriorate rapidly. This caused Esther great anxiety but she made him as comfortable as possible, wrapped in his rug in the now comfortably warm room, and prayed that he wouldn't get any worse. She had no car, or no telephone, so recognised that she was totally dependent on God, in yet another testing situation.

At half-past seven that evening Esther heard another car stop outside the front door. It was Ruth back to introduce Jim to Trevor and her. She was glad to see them for she was becoming increasingly concerned about Darren and it would be reassuring to have somebody to talk to until Trevor came back, if they could stay.

When the visitors followed Esther into the living room Darren was still all wrapped up and looking distinctly distressed. He was obviously finding it very difficult to breathe.

Jim and Ruth had just been in about half-an-hour when Esther decided to put the boys to bed. With Gregory settled first she returned to the room for Darren. As he was struggling to make it out to the bedroom, Ruth observed, "Esther that wee boy is very sick."

It wasn't long until her declaration of concern was proved to be correct. Darren's mum had just returned to join the others for a short time and was beginning to find out a little about them when her 'wee boy' appeared back beside her, looking wretched.

"Mummy, when I lie down I can't breathe, " he gasped. "My chest is very sore."

When Ruth saw the state he was in she realised that he needed help. "Come on, Esther," she said, with the air of someone about to set out on an urgent undertaking. "We will go into my house and phone the doctor."

"But we haven't registered with a doctor yet," Esther protested.

"That doesn't make any difference," Ruth replied. "We will phone ours. That child needs to be seen tonight."

Although it was difficult to leave Darren behind with Jim, Esther recognised that her new friend was right. She had no alternative. They went to Ruth's house, called her doctor and returned to Darren as soon as possible.

When he had heard Esther describe her twelve-year-old son's condition the doctor promised to be out with him straightaway. The two ladies had just returned to the house and hadn't yet settled down before the fire again when he arrived.

By this time Darren's breathing had become very loud and rapid. The doctor entered the room, looked over to where he was struggling to get a breath, and pronounced immediately, "This young lad will have to go into Magherafelt Hospital. Can you take him in if I ring them and tell them you are coming?"

Esther said that she could, assuming correctly that Ruth would be willing to drive Darren and her into the hospital in town.

This decision left Esther in a predicament. She would have to leave Gregory, who was fast asleep, and unaware of all that was going on around him, in the charge of a man she had just met that evening and whom Gregory would barely know if he wakened up.

There was no other way out, though.

Darren had to be taken into the hospital without delay. And it was also essential that she should be with him.

Jim assured Esther that he would be quite able to handle Gregory if he awoke. With that she and Ruth set off to the local hospital with Darren for urgent treatment.

They were some time away and in their absence Trevor arrived home. He drove up to the back of the bungalow without the slightest inkling that anything had changed since he left. There were no cars around so Esther and the boys would probably be in on their own.

The returning husband and father came in through the kitchen and on in towards the living room to see how everyone was, but his main concern at that moment was for Darren. Meanwhile Jim had heard the car stop in the yard, and was on his way out to see who was arriving.

The two men who had never met each other in their lives before came face to face in the living room doorway.

Trevor was taken aback. He had been expecting Esther to greet him, but who was this totally unknown person obviously making himself comfortable in their house? And where was his wife?

The stranger realised that Trevor would be worried at seeing him and so at once began to account for his presence. "Hello there, I take it you must be Trevor," he said. "You don't know me, but I'm Jim. You met my wife Ruth a couple of days ago. We called over to see you this evening after church but Darren was so bad that the two women have taken him in to Magherafelt Hospital."

An appreciable wall of anxiety and awkwardness was broken down with that simple explanation. Trevor stretched out his hand and as they shook hands warmly, greeted the stand-in baby-sitter with, "Pleased to meet you, Jim. Now tell me what all happened this evening."

They sat down together and when Jim had recounted the story of Darren's deteriorating condition, the phone call, the doctor and the hospital, Trevor decided that he should follow Ruth and Esther into the hospital to see how they were all doing.

He was still preparing to leave the house, though, when the two women returned with the news that Darren had been given steroids and put on a nebulizer. He had been admitted to hospital but the staff were confident that he could be stabilised and should recover quickly. They were right in their prediction for by Tuesday afternoon Darren was ready to be discharged.

When Trevor and Esther had collected him from hospital and were driving home they began to recall the events of the previous few days. They were both thankful to God for His provision of new friends. It was clear that He had sent both Wray and Kathleen and Jim and Ruth to help them through a most trying weekend.

The lovely couple had met two other lovely couples.

24

PLEASE DON'T MAKE ME LAUGH!

The following Sunday was September 29 and the date when Trevor was due to commence his first Gospel campaign as a full-time worker with The Faith Mission. Although Esther and he would have liked to be working together, the Mission had agreed that each of them should conduct his or her first meetings in conjunction with more experienced workers. Trevor had been teamed with Robert Orr, who was the mission leader, and another graduate, Robert Murdock.

He was in absolute agony as he was preparing to leave the house late that afternoon. The pain in his back had grown steadily worse and he was now finding it extremely difficult to move around. When it came time to go he had to reach out and use both hands to swing his right leg into the car. As he drove along between Magherafelt and Broughshane the pain became even more excruciating.

On arriving at the hall where he was due to take part in his first mission meeting as a Faith Mission worker, he just managed to struggle out of the car and hobble, bent double, across to a nearby five-barred gate.

As people started to arrive for the meeting many of them passed Trevor, whom they expected to be one of the speakers that evening, as he had been introduced to them the previous Sunday, hanging on to a gate as though his life depended on it.

"Are you not coming in?" some of them enquired, puzzled that he should have chosen to stand outside when everyone else seemed to be happy to make towards the relative warmth and comfort of the hall. They gathered from his tortured expression that something was the matter, but Trevor tried to answer such concerned queries with a, "No. Not just yet. I may be in later."

There was only an outside chance of that happening, however.

He told the two Roberts that he wouldn't be able to come into the meeting. It would be difficult to sit on a wooden seat for any length of time and absolutely impossible to step up onto a platform.

Trevor was thoroughly disappointed not to be taking part on the opening night of his first scheduled Gospel mission. This disappointment was compounded as people continued to file past him in a steady stream on their way into the hall.

How he wished that he could be going in too.

He couldn't, though, for even the slightest movement shot bolts of unbearable pain up his back and down into his legs.

When he heard the congregation singing in the hall he knew that the meeting had begun and so there would hopefully be fewer mystified passers-by. He stood for ten more minutes and then decided to try and make his way down the road to the prayer caravan. The chill of the autumn night was beginning to penetrate his body so it would be better if he could make it indoors somewhere. And he had to be out of the way before the meeting ended. It was bad enough standing hanging on to a gate when they were going in, but if he was still there when they came out what would they think?

The caravan that was to be used for prayer meetings during the mission was only about two hundred yards down the road but the walk to it was one of the most agonizing expeditions Trevor had ever embarked upon. Every step was a nightmare. No part of his body wanted to move. He was stiff, sore and in unbelievable pain.

When he reached the caravan eventually it was a mammoth task to stretch up and unlock the door. Having managed to pull the door open his next obstacle was to get up the step and into the caravan. He did this virtually on hands and knees, and when inside he clambered on to one of the long seats that could be used as a bed, to see if he could possibly gain any ease.

Lying still meant that he didn't aggravate the pain and send it darting through his body. It didn't put it away though.

When Trevor heard the congregation dispersing after the meeting and saw the succession of car headlights send an eerie light through the caravan as they drove off down the road, for he hadn't been able to draw the curtains, he realised that help would soon be at hand.

Surely the two Roberts would come and find him.

They did, after they had seen the last person out of the hall. It had only been twenty minutes but it seemed like two hours to tortured Trevor.

When senior and junior Robert stepped up into the caravan they were initially all taken up with the apparent success of the first night of the mission. There had been, they said, 'a good crowd in for the opening night,' and there had also been 'a great feeling in the meeting.' They reported this to Trevor in response to his enquiry, "Well boys, how did it go?"

When Robert Orr saw the effort it had taken for his young colleague to ask that question he became immediately concerned and came back with a query of his own. "And how are you?" he was anxious to know.

"In desperate pain, to be honest with you," Trevor replied. "I have no idea how I am ever going to get off this bed."

"Don't worry, Trevor," Robert reassured him. "I will drive you home in my car and Robert junior can follow behind in yours."

That proved to be easier said than done, however.

When Trevor tried to rise to go home he found that he just couldn't move. It seemed as though all his joints had locked. He slid sideways off the bed onto the floor where he remained on his hands and knees, seized up, rigid.

The two Roberts began to discuss how they were 'going to get Trevor out of here and into the car.' At one point Robert Orr suggested, "If we could go out to some of the farms round here we could maybe find a big board, like a door or something, to lay him on. Then we could carry him out on it."

It was impossible, but all three of them found the prospect of it particularly funny. Trevor began to laugh. "How do you think you could get me flattened out on to a board?" he chortled. "I don't even bend. And how would you plan to bring a door into this confined space? Or worse still manoeuvre it out again with me on it?"

The two aspiring paramedics ended up in fits of laughter. Since laughter is often infectious, Trevor began to laugh at them laughing at him, and this made his pain far worse.

"Oh please don't make me laugh!" he begged.

When they had calmed down they decided that their only hope of moving Trevor out into the car was to lift him gently by the armpits and half-carry half-trail him out. Trevor found it extremely painful to put either foot to the ground, and only did so when he had to.

It took half-an-hour of pain for Trevor and persuasion from his two helpers to see him out into the car. When he was safely deposited in the front seat of Robert Orr's car they drove directly to Magherafelt Hospital. All three were agreed that Trevor could not be allowed to go home in such absolute misery.

When they were seen in the Accident and Emergency Unit at the hospital the doctor asked Trevor to remove all his outer clothes. This was a further exercise in agony. After a thorough examination the doctor gave him an injection into his back to relieve the pain.

Robert Orr and Robert Murdock sat waiting for him for a long time. What they didn't know was that Trevor was stuck in a cubicle trying desperately to put on his socks. He still couldn't bend over.

There was more hilarity when they returned, eventually, to Trevor's home. Esther offered her husband's chauffeur and his assistant a cup of tea and as they were sitting around in the kitchen they began to recount the events of the evening. One of the men described Trevor 'on the floor on all fours, powerless and motionless, like a paralysed frog.' The other added to that by remarking, through his giggles, "We thought we were going to have to cut a hole in the roof, like they did for the man in the Bible. Then we could bring in a crane from somewhere to lift him out!"

The only one of the four not sitting down was Trevor. Although the pain had begun to ease slightly with the injection he still stood with his hands spread out flat on the worktops for support.

"Oh please don't make me laugh!" he pleaded for the second time that evening. 'Please, please, don't make me laugh!"

The worst of the pain was soon to pass, however. The injection proved most effective and on Tuesday night Trevor was able to return to the mission in Ballygelly, and by Friday night he was well enough to preach for the first time.

People from the district continued to come along to the meetings in the following weeks and one Saturday night Trevor had the thrill of leading a husband and wife to faith in Christ.

The mission that had begun with Trevor in physical pain was to end with him having achieved a sense of the fulfilment of spiritual purpose. That was why he and Esther had been called to attend Bible College and enter the work of The Faith Mission. They were genuinely keen to see others experience the joy and satisfaction that salvation had brought to them.

A week after Trevor's mission came to an end Esther began her first spell in an outreach campaign as a Faith Mission worker in early November 1991. In keeping with the Mission's policy she was placed with two more experienced workers, Esther Hewitt and Anna Morrison.

The three of them were to conduct their campaign in the Mission Hall in Balnamore, a village a few miles outside Ballymoney in County Antrim. Esther was pleased at this, her first posting, for she counted it an honour to be assigned to work alongside Esther Hewitt, a prominent and popular preacher in the Mission.

The first week of the campaign was to be devoted to Christian teaching, and the three ladies involved agreed that they would take it in turns to speak for as long as the entire mission lasted. This meant that each of them was responsible for presenting the message every third evening.

Trevor and Esther had long since discovered that evangelical outreach consisted of more than just preaching at a meeting in the evening, though. One of the worker's most important roles was in visitation. He or she would be expected to call at all the homes in the neighbourhood with a personal invitation to the local meetings.

Attending for visitation in the Balnamore mission presented Esther with a transport issue, which in turn was to have a knock-on effect on her husband, before it was satisfactorily resolved. She, at that time, did not have a valid driving licence for Northern Ireland, and so Trevor had to leave her to the mission location every day and then return to Magherafelt to meet the boys coming out of school. Anna then drove her home in the evening after the meeting.

This, to all those involved, wasn't looked upon as a problem. It was more of a privilege, to be together in the service of the Lord.

Esther threw herself into the work of this mission with a will, engaging in the daily programme of visitation and speaking in the Children's Bible Clubs and the evening services.

She was tremendously encouraged when the message she had prepared for just her second meeting in the mission, during the Christian teaching week, touched the heart of a lady in the audience. Esther had entitled her theme for that evening 'The Potter and the Clay,' based on the first few verses of Jeremiah chapter eight in the Bible. In the course of her address she asked the question, "Have you got off the Potter's wheel before He has finished with you?"

This challenged a woman in the congregation and on the way out she asked if she could possibly speak to one of the workers. Esther Hewitt was happy to take her into the little back room for counselling, and in the course of conversation Gloria confessed that she had in fact spun off the Potter's wheel. She was a Christian but for the past number of years hadn't been living as she should, and thus had ceased to enjoy the peace of knowing the presence of God in her life. The experienced Esther read the scriptures with her and as they prayed together Gloria was restored to the joy of her salvation. Esther junior was delighted to learn of Gloria's restoration and constantly heartened by her attendance at nearly all the succeeding meetings in Balnamore.

Having each served with more seasoned campaigners as required, Trevor and Esther assumed that they must have 'passed their test' when they were permitted to conduct their first mission together in February 1992.

This was to be held in a hall in the townland of Ballymoughan, which was on the outskirts of Magherafelt and less than two miles from their own home. They prayed together, and with the local Christians, about this challenge and opportunity that had been presented to them. They then set out on a programme of visitation before the mission was due to commence, calling on every home within a wide radius.

God seemed to answer the many prayers He had heard for the mission, and at least some of the local people appeared ready to respond to the personal invitation, which they had received on their doorstep or in their farmyard.

The hall was full on the opening night, and the numbers of those attending increased with every meeting. By the middle of the second week there were so many people coming along that seating had become a major problem. Chairs had to be borrowed and placed in every available spot just to get all the people seated.

It wasn't just the numbers of people coming to the meetings that was growing, either. As God's blessing became evident in salvation, almost from the start of the mission, the fervour and earnestness of the local Christians increased as well. They were beset with a desire to pray for their friends and neighbours.

It seemed strange, but it was an example of how God was working in the district, that the actual holding of one of those prayer meetings led a man to consider coming to Christ.

Tommy Johnston is a farmer, and one cold winter morning he was going out at half-past six in the morning to commence his day's work. He looked across his fields and was impressed to see that the light was on in the hall where the mission was being held. Tommy had been to the meetings a few times and had heard either Trevor or Esther encourage the Christians to join them, 'at half-six tomorrow morning to pray.'

The Lord said to him, as he stood there in his own yard, "Those people over there have come out at this time in the morning to pray for you." The thought went straight to his heart. If these people were so concerned about him, why was he not doing something about his soul?

He decided that he would take action there and then. Tommy retraced his steps into the house and on up to the bedroom that he hadn't long left. There he fell down on his knees and accepted the Lord Jesus as his Saviour.

What the two mission leaders found thrilling about this was that they didn't hear the news of Tommy's conversion directly from him at first. It was a couple of his nephews who phoned at different times during the day to let them know. Tommy had been in touch with them, and many more besides, to tell them he had come to Christ. This was in keeping with what Trevor and Esther had been telling their packed audiences every night. 'If you have got saved, make sure and tell somebody. The Bible says we are not only to believe in our hearts but also to confess with our mouths, for salvation...'

Soon the news of that mission had spread far and wide. People were weeping openly in the meetings. Someone was being led to faith in Christ almost every evening.

Trevor and Esther were both happy and humbled to have experienced what they considered to be the seal of God on their combined ministry.

Many of the local Christians were convinced that He had led the dedicated young couple into their area and was using them to bring 'a real sense of revival' to Ballymoughan.

And could there possibly be even more blessing to come?

25

IT'S NOT BUTTER I WANT!

Such was the tide of blessing that had begun to flow that it was to last not only for the duration of that mission but also for years to come, both in Ballymoughan and elsewhere. The formation of a weekly Prayer Union in the district was one of the evident lasting spiritual benefits to accrue from it. With the local Christians having become so fired-up for God, and so many recent converts just longing to grow in their faith, the newly established Ballymoughan Prayer Union was enthusiastically supported from its inception.

Following hard on the exhilarating times of spiritual refreshing in their first combined mission Trevor and Esther moved just a few miles across country to Ballymaguiggan Mission Hall. This was at the invitation of Jim Jamieson, who had requested that they come to the Hall, even prior to the days of blessing witnessed in Ballymoughan.

During this second gospel outreach in the Magherafelt area Trevor and Esther had asked Trevor Matthews, Faith Mission

Superintendent, to be their guest speaker one Wednesday evening. He chose as his scripture text the lament of King David at the death of Abner from 2 Samuel chapter three. The question, which he repeated often in the course of his address was, 'Died Abner as a fool dieth?'

The message touched home to the hearts of a couple in the meeting for on the following evening a lady, who introduced herself as Shirley, said to Trevor, "My husband and I were both here last night and we were wondering if you and your wife would be free to come round to talk to us tomorrow night after the meeting? We would like to get right with God."

That was the sort of an invitation that Trevor and Esther loved to receive, and which they never refused, and the following night, after the service, they accompanied Shirley round to her home. When they arrived they found that her husband, Ian, was waiting for them there.

Shirley, who appeared by far the more outgoing of the two, was the first to express her desire to come to know the Lord. It was obvious to her two visitors that she was actively seeking salvation. Esther talked to her, and after they had read some relevant scriptures together, Shirley trusted in Christ.

Trevor then turned to Ian. It had never been his practice to buttonhole anybody, but on this occasion, since Shirley had asked him to come round to speak to both of them, he made an exception.

"And what about you, Ian?" he enquired, hoping that Shirley's husband would be as ready to speak his mind as she had been to open up on her desire to know peace in her soul. It seemed that he wasn't, however.

Ian Booth, although a burly big man, turned out to be painfully shy. He appeared reluctant to say anything. The longest sentence he was able to manage was about four words. And that was after prolonged hesitation, and with a great deal of effort.

Assuming, then that Shirley had been right, and that Ian was, despite his reticence, anxious to 'get right with God,' he tried a different tack.

He resorted to asking him questions that required only one-word answers, and thus he led him to the Lord.

Both Ian and Shirley were soon rejoicing in their newly found faith and they never missed a meeting for the remainder of the mission. It wasn't long either until the formerly extremely self-conscious Ian was volunteering to help in the meeting in any way that he could.

Before the end of the meetings in Ballymaguiggan Ian asked Trevor if he would go round to see his father, Robert. Now that he was saved himself he was concerned that his dad and other members of the family should come to faith in Christ as well.

Trevor did as Ian requested and Ian's father began attending some meetings in that and subsequent missions, seeming at times moved by the messages he heard. Then, mysteriously, he stopped coming. Months passed, and Trevor and Esther began to wonder what had happened to Robert.

Their opportunity to make contact with him again arose in a somewhat unusual manner. One morning Jim Jamieson arrived up at the front of their house in the car, looking for some advice. At that time the EEC had decided to share its 'butter mountain' with some of the more needy members of the community and prominent figures in society, including church leaders, had been asked to help with the distribution.

"I have a box of EEC butter in the boot of the car here, Trevor," Jim began. "I have given some of it out but have still more than half a box of it left. Have you any ideas about who I should give it to?"

"What about going around some of the people who used to come along to our recent missions, but have stopped, and we seem to have lost touch with them," Trevor suggested, after a minute or twos thought. " I mean people like Robert Booth, for example."

Having agreed that this was 'a good idea,' Jim left the house and half an hour later he was on the telephone to Trevor. He sounded all of a fluster.

"Do you know what happened when I went to Robert Booth's door with the butter?" he said, his voice trembling with an undisguised spiritual excitement. Without waiting for Trevor to respond with the obvious, 'No, What?' Jim continued, "He looked at me with a tear in his eye and burst out, 'It's not butter I want! It's salvation!'"

Trevor realised immediately why Jim sounded so delighted. He left what he was doing and drove over to Robert's home. When he arrived Robert met him with a smile.

"Jim probably told you what I said to him," he began, recognising the connection between his visitors at once. "But what I have to tell you is that when he left I got down on my knees and confessed my sin. I then asked Jesus to come into my heart and change my life." Trevor stayed with him for another hour as they both gave thanks to God that Robert had received something better than butter.

Incidents like this, when it was evident that God was at work, answering the prayers of His people, continued to occur, and served to heighten the spiritual fervour in the area. It was in this climate of the manifest blessing of the Lord, too, that Trevor and Esther were informed that The Faith Mission were extending their term of service in the Magherafelt district.

In May 1992 Trevor and Esther were invited to conduct a mission in Coagh, County Tyrone. The men from the local Christian Fellowship helped them procure the use of a site from the Housing Executive, on which to erect a portable hall. A number of other local Christians joined the men of the Fellowship in preparing the site, putting up the hall and praying continuously for 'the forthcoming meetings.'

It was very clear, right from the commencement of those meetings, that the 'showers of blessing' that had begun to fall way back in Ballymoughan, over a year before were set to continue, and even develop perhaps into a more prolonged period of 'spiritual rain from heaven.'

So many people began to come that by the middle of the first week the hall, which had been so carefully erected, couldn't hold the crowds who were coming to hear the Gospel. With the provision of extra accommodation a pressing and major, but nonetheless welcome, hurdle to have to overcome, some of the local Christians suggested that Trevor should approach Jim Henry, a local businessman, who used Portacabins. He did this, and Jim came up with a very innovative solution.

The residents of Coagh were astonished to witness, one afternoon, a long truck draw up with a Portacabin on the trailer. This was followed by a mobile crane, and the villagers stood spellbound as the crane lifted the temporary room high in the air to swing it round and place it in at the back of 'the wee hall.'

When this was connected up to the existing building the accommodation was more than doubled, and still they had difficulty getting the people in. The delivery of an extension by mobile crane had caused such a buzz of excitement in the district many came to the mission out of curiosity, just 'to see what was going on.' The weather was warm during the mission, and with the doors and windows open those who couldn't find a place inside the halls either stood or sat around outside, listening.

On Sunday June 7, the power of God was demonstrated in a mighty and unmistakeable way, during and following the afternoon meeting.

It was Esther's turn to speak that day, and the presence of God became so real to all present, that many began to weep. At the close of the meeting those who had been overcome by an awareness of their need of salvation remained in their seats to await counselling.

Before he returned to commence speaking to one of those waiting to be seen by either Esther or himself, Trevor went down to the door to shake hands with the people who were leaving. And it was then that he met Lorraine.

The tears were streaming down the woman's cheeks, but from the smell of her breath and the slurring of her speech when she spoke to him, Trevor realised that she was drunk. "You must call down to see me," she begged. "Will you promise to come down to see me?"

Trevor said that he and Esther would call down at her house, which was close to the hall, as soon as they were free. The young couple responsible for the preaching in the meetings were constantly appreciative of the practical support of the believers from the surrounding area, and in this case, their wisdom and care was very evident.

Just as Lorraine was leaving the hall Eunice Gibson, the local Prayer Union leader, stepped forward. "Don't worry, Lorraine, I'll go down and stay with you until Trevor and Esther are ready," she volunteered, and with that she escorted Lorraine, a well-known alcoholic, back to her house.

It was to be almost two hours before Trevor and Esther were ready, however. There were so many people waiting patiently in the hall, and the mission leaders dealt with each person in turn, reading and praying with every one of them, until they had seen them all led to faith in Christ.

When they eventually emerged into the early evening it was still hot and Trevor and Esther were encouraged to find that many of the Christians had remained outside the hall. They were well aware that the Spirit of God was moving in the hearts of many people and had wanted to remain and support the work in prayer, or however else they may be needed.

One or two of them asked, "Are you going down to see Lorraine now?" When either Trevor or Esther answered in the affirmative the response was always the same, "We will be praying for you."

As they were approaching the door Esther whispered to her husband, "This woman's drunk. What are we going to say to her?"

When Trevor and Esther went into the house the others who had been sitting in with Lorraine left and the door had barely closed behind them, when Lorraine, who was still clearly, 'under the influence,' came straight to the point.

"I was in the meeting on Friday night, Esther, when you spoke about the broad way and the narrow way, and I have asked you to come down here tonight because I want to get saved, " she said, virtually all in one breath, and surprisingly fluently.

Trevor and Esther looked across at one another. They said nothing but the look that passed between them seemed to ask the unspoken question, "Can God save a drunk woman?"

They hesitated, neither of them quite sure what to say, thus each left it to the other with the result that neither of them spoke. Lorraine was in earnest, though, and conscious of what was either incredulity or indecision on their part, decided to initiate the proceedings herself.

"All right!" she exclaimed. "If you don't want to pray with me then I'll do it myself!" and with that she threw herself down on the floor.

The two counsellors were soon down with her, one on either side. Their unvoiced question had been dramatically answered. Yes. God could save a drunk woman, and if He was about to, they were willing to play their part, under His direction.

They talked to her of sin, of God and His love, and about the death of Christ on the cross for her sin, and His desire to be her Saviour. When they had explained all this Lorraine committed her life to Christ, lying on her own living room floor. Trevor then prayed and thanked the Lord for her salvation.

When he had finished Lorraine leapt up from her prone position to standing tall, all in one startling, athletic movement. She then stretched her arms up into the air and proclaimed repeatedly, "I'm clean! I'm clean! I'm clean!"

As Trevor and Esther were picking themselves up from the floor, and before they had time to say anything more to the exuberant new convert, she started to dash around the house.

"What are you doing, Lorraine?" Esther asked.

"Don't worry," came the reply. "You'll soon see."

They did, too, and they not only saw, but smelt the next act in the swiftly moving drama. Lorraine had started to make a systematic tour of the house, collecting bottles of vodka from all the hidey-holes where she had them stashed, and then coming to pour them down the sink.

Esther quipped to her awestruck husband at one stage, "It's a good job you can't get drunk on the smell of that stuff, or we would both be away with it."

Ten minutes later Lorraine came to join her two counsellors in the living room, having the appearance of someone who had just completed a very rewarding job.

"Is that it all, Lorraine?" Trevor enquired.

"Yes, Trevor, that's it all this time. I've tried to give it up before, but always kept a bottle or two hidden away, just in case," Lorraine replied. "But that's it all this time. Every single drop of it! I'm saved! I'm saved!"

The amazing thing was that Lorraine, who was patently drunk when they arrived into her home, was by then perfectly sober. And what was more, the whites of her eyes, which had become a cloudy yellow colour, had begun to turn white again!

When she was leaving Trevor and Esther to the door some time later, all three of them were pleasantly surprised to find that a number of the praying Christians were still around and a time of great rejoicing ensued.

Next day Lorraine told all the non-Christians she met in the street that she had got saved. Everyone in the village knew her, and the problem she had experienced with alcohol addiction, so the most common response to her public confession of her faith was, "That's great, Lorraine. Congratulations. You certainly needed it!"

Perhaps the most poignant tribute to the power of God to change a life, and one that brought a lump to Trevor's throat every time he thought of it for a long time afterwards, came when he was visiting in Lorraine's home, a few days later.

He was just about to leave, when one of Lorraine's children, all of whom had been used to fending for themselves and going without for years, while their mum satisfied her craving for alcohol, crept up beside him.

"Thank you, mister," she whispered. "We've got a new mammy!"

Coagh, Trevor reckoned at that moment would have been worth it all, even if Lorraine had been the only one to come to faith in Christ.

She hadn't been, though.

There were many others as well.

26

THE TENT'S DOWN AND TREVOR'S DEAD!

Preaching consistently, night after night, soon began to take its toll on Esther's voice. Her throat became constantly sore, her voice croaky and raspy.

Trevor recognised this, even before she started to consider it a problem, and said to her on the way home from a meeting one evening, "Esther, we really need a microphone." His wife agreed, as it would ease the strain on both their voices. Trevor told her that he would 'make a few enquires some of these days', to see what was available.

When he called in with John Palmer, a trader in Moneymore, one Monday morning he was shown a public address system that would be ideal for their use. John explained that it had been ordered for a church, but when they saw it, discovered that it did not meet their specific needs.

A purchase price was agreed and Trevor paid John a deposit,

adding that he would call in 'and square him up for the rest,' before the end of the week. It was a bold statement. It was a statement of faith, for neither Esther nor he had the amount of money required to pay off this outstanding debt. On the way home in the car, with his new P.A, system in the boot, Trevor prayed to God, who had met their every need before, to meet this one.

The next night a lady stopped with Esther at the door on her way into the meeting. "That's a personal gift for Trevor and yourself from the Cookstown Prayer Union," she whispered, and passed an envelope into her hand.

Esther's heart pounded. As she stood there, holding this 'personal gift,' she knew immediately in her heart that God had provided them with the means to pay off the P.A. system. She told Trevor about it as they were driving home and they weren't long into the house until she began to investigate the contents of the envelope.

This is odd, she thought, as she emptied all that was in it out on to a table. Personal gifts to them usually came in the form of cheques, or cash in neat multiples of five or ten pounds. This, however, was an uneven sum, and it included a number of coins. It looked to her as though it had been a collection taken up at a meeting somewhere and then handed on to them in its entirety.

The amazing thing was that when Trevor and Esther had counted the money, and then deducted their tithe from it, they discovered that Esther's conviction had been correct. What remained was enough to cover the outstanding bill for the P.A. system. And it was the required amount, right down to the very last pound. £167 exactly!

Not only was God saving souls, but He was also continuing to provide for His servants, with amazing and absolute precision.

Their new public address unit was put to good use during the tent mission, which began on Sunday, April 25, 1993, at The Grange, near Magherafelt. A team of six had been assigned to conduct that particular outreach campaign. Trevor and Esther, and David and Marjorie Bennett were to be the main speakers. Robert Orr and Robert Simpson, who took responsibility for arranging a programme of meetings amongst the children, assisted them in the preaching from time to time.

The mission had only been going a week and many people had started to come along. Christians from a wide radius attended to register their support for the effort and a number of the local people had dropped in on occasional evenings out of mere curiosity. It was all looking very promising when a calamity occurred.

Trevor awoke at six o'clock one morning to find that a storm had arisen during the night and that a gale was howling around the house. He immediately thought of the tent. Could it possibly have survived?

When he couldn't bear the suspense of not knowing whether or not they were going to have a tent in which to hold their meeting that night any longer he slid out of bed. "I'm going over to see if the tent's all right," he told Esther. "There is a terrible storm going on out there. It could be in shreds."

Having dressed hastily Trevor drove across to The Grange, only to discover that his worst fears had been realised. Ernie Campbell, one of the mission organisers, had already arrived on the site, having been alerted by a passing motorist on his way to work, and they began to assess the damage.

In less than an hour after leaving home Trevor phoned back to Esther with some less than encouraging news. His wife felt that sinking feeling in her stomach when he began to report, "The tent's down, Esther, and it's going to be some job to fix it. One of the poles is broken, for a start. And there is a fifteen foot rip in one of canvas sections and a seven or eight foot rip in another. Ernie is here with me and we are going across to his house now to call David and Marjorie and the two Roberts to let them know. Then we will have to work out some way to have it repaired before tonight."

Before they left the site Trevor and Ernie secured everything in and around the tent, for it was still blowing a gale. They then loosened the ropes and dropped the tent to prevent any further damage, before Trevor headed off with Ernie, back to his house, to formulate a plan of action over an earlier than usual breakfast. They could never have anticipated what consternation this simple move was to provoke, however!

George and Helen Caldwell lived in a bungalow at the edge of the field in which the tent had been pitched, and had attended the meetings a few nights out of interest. In doing that, they had come to know Trevor and Esther, and also quite incidentally, that they drove a dark grey Volkswagen Jetta.

On the morning after the night of the storm Helen pulled up her kitchen blind only to witness the scene of destruction. It was awful to see that the tent was down and shreds of canvas were waving pathetically in the strong wind, but something else, which she considered to be even scarier, struck her. Trevor's car was there, but he most certainly wasn't in it, and he wasn't to be seen anywhere.

Helen was immediately overcome by an inexplicable sense of doom and rushed straight to the telephone. She knew that Ernie Campbell 'took a lot to do with the mission,' and so she rang him.

"Oh Ernie, you'd better come quickly," she burst out, as soon as she heard his voice at the other end of the line. "The tent's down and Trevor's dead! His car's here but he is nowhere to be seen."

Much to Helen's surprise, Ernie immediately burst out laughing. "Don't worry Helen," he tried to console her, when he had composed himself. "The tent's down right enough, but Trevor's not dead. He's here with me, sitting at his breakfast! I met him over there about an hour ago and we decided to come to my house for a bite to eat and to make a few phone calls. Rest assured, Trevor's O.K. and we will be back over to the field to start work again soon."

As news spread that the tent had blown down Christians from around the area began to gravitate towards the site. One of them heard a neighbour who lived farther up the lane past the Caldwell's bungalow remark as he was passing on the way to work, "That's definitely the end of the mission. That tent's ruined. They'll never get it fixed!"

The willing band of workers who had gathered around the stricken tent had other ideas, however. It was the Bank Holiday weekend, and this was good news in one sense, bad news in another. The positive aspect was that many of the men who would normally have been at work, were actually on holiday, and therefore available to assist in the repair operation. The downer was that all the firms, which they would wish to contact for help and advice, were closed for the day.

Their first problem was the torn canvas. Some of the mission organisers contacted the management of Cunningham Covers in Tobermore, just six miles away, and found them very helpful and most reassuring. Holiday or no holiday they said, "Don't you worry. Get the canvas to us and we will mend it for you. We don't mind a bit of a challenge!"

Some of the men soon organised a lorry to take the torn sections across to Cunningham's and that was the first of their problems solved. The next one might prove a lot more difficult, though. How, or where, did you procure a brand new tent pole on a Bank Holiday with every timber yard you could think of round the country closed?

It was then that Robert Orr came up with a novel idea. "Why not cut down a tree?" he suggested. Trevor and the others reckoned that this was a proposal worth considering but it, in turn, raised a couple of different problems. Where, for example, would you find a suitably straight tree, and how would you know which one would be the right height to suit the purpose?

One of the men on the site contacted someone with access to trees, explained the situation, and obtained permission to cut down a tree in a nearby forest. How, though, would they know which tree to choose?

Again Robert had the answer. "We can measure the broken pole, and then we will know what height of a one we will need," he told the team of men who had agreed that they could soon fell a tree. Their only difficulty would be to choose one of the proper length.

"I read, somewhere," Robert went on to explain, " that if you know what height of a tree you want, you walk that distance away from the base of the tree, stop, and bend down to look between your legs at the top of it. If you can't see the tip of the tree from that position then it will be long enough for you, apparently."

Some of the men rolled their eyes at this rule-of-thumb trigonometry, but decided that in the circumstances anything was worth a try. The team set off, armed with two chain saws, to put Robert's formula, about which some of them were still mildly sceptical, into practice

Much to their astonishment, and Robert's amusement at their astonishment, however, it worked! The volunteer lumberjacks cut down the selected spruce and when they had stripped it of all its branches and then its bark, they transported it to the site on a long trailer. The big test then was to try it for height and when they did so found that it was only four inches too long! A single stroke of the saw left it trimmed to size and ready for use!

The men were still in the process of measuring the pole and putting it into place when another trailer drew up at the field from Cunningham Covers in Tobermore. They were returning the canvas, expertly repaired.

By four-thirty that afternoon, when the man from up the lane was coming home from work, the tent had been re-erected and was being prepared for the evening meeting. The field seemed full of busy, happy Christians laughing with, and chatting to one another as they worked away together.

"I would never have believed it possible!" was all the dumbfounded neighbour could gasp. He was virtually speechless, and conceded that he had witnessed 'a modern miracle.'

God rewarded the perseverance of all those diligent workers who had rallied around to put the tent up again after the storm, for many were to come to the Saviour during that mission. Three of those were George and Helen Caldwell and their daughter, Sarah, from the bungalow beside the tent.

Trevor found Helen's salvation particularly gratifying.

The woman, who had once concluded that he was dead, had now found new life in Christ!

27

NO MORE JAM!

In January 1994 Trevor and Esther received a letter from The Faith Mission asking them if they would consider moving to Cork as area workers. They gave this suggestion some prayerful consideration and decided that even though they seemed to be experiencing the blessing of God in every mission, it was probably time to move on to another location, in His service. If the Mission felt that Cork was the place where their abilities could best be utilised, then they would be quite happy to go to Cork.

There was much work to be done, however, before their proposed move to the most southerly city in Ireland during the coming summer.

A spring mission had been planned in Tullygrawley outside Ballymena in County Antrim, and as was Trevor and Esther's custom prior to, and during every mission, they began an intensive programme of visitation in the district. They always aimed to make a personal call at every home to invite people along.

This time, though, despite feeling that they were well organised and had covered the area thoroughly, they somehow missed out on one particular home. The house was up a little lane on the Teeshan Road.

Although Trevor and Esther didn't know that the lane with the house at the end of it was there, God did, and He had made preparations, through another of His children, to contact the family living there. David Logan knew the Mc Kendry family, Ed and Claire and the children well, and contacted them to ask if they would be interested in coming along to the mission.

Davy, as everybody knew him, called repeatedly at the home but the only response to his invitation came from little Mark, Ed and Claire's six year-old-son. Mark came along with the kind neighbour on a number of occasions and every night, as he was getting out of Davy's car he said, "I'm going to try and get my daddy to come with us some night."

That was exactly what Davy wanted too, and eventually Ed consented to go along. Little Mark was delighted that his dad had come and when Ed arrived home he said to his wife, "You ought to go and hear that couple sometime, Claire. They are good." That was fine to say, but what neither Claire, Davy, Mark or anybody else knew was that Ed had decided he wasn't going back. He had gone once to please them all. Surely that should be enough.

About a week later Claire responded to Davy's invitation, and taking her husband's advice went along to 'hear that couple.' What happened that evening was amazing, for in her first meeting she heard a stirring Gospel message and didn't leave the hall until she had trusted in Christ as her Saviour.

Ed, though, had determined that he wasn't going back. Salvation might be all right for Claire, but he reckoned it wasn't for him. Davy wasn't prepared to give up, however, and one afternoon he thought he would pay Ed a visit, to invite him once again. Ed had seen him coming as he was tinkering with an old car in the yard, so he issued little Mark, who was playing nearby, with the terse instruction, "If Davy is looking for me, tell him I'm down the fields." He then slid in below the car and lay still.

Sure enough, when the godly man stepped out of his car his first enquiry was for Ed, and Mark informed him that he wasn't about. He was 'down the fields.'

Davy told his little friend not to worry for he would call and see his dad again sometime. He then arranged to pick Mark up for the meeting that evening, and left.

When Ed crawled out from below the car he was free from Davy until he 'called again sometime' but he was soon to find that he wasn't free of something else. That was his conscience.

What kind of a low-down father are you, it accused, that you would actually expect your young son to tell a lie, just to save yourself from having to make some kind of an excuse to a good Christian man for not going along to a Gospel meeting ?

There was no escaping it either. Every time he looked at Mark his conscience pricked him once more. There was only one way to relieve himself of this stigma, he decided. Next time Davy called to invite him to the meetings he would go.

He didn't have to wait long, either. A few days later Davy was back in the yard, but this time Ed was up and about and happy to be seen. When Davy asked him to go to the meeting with him that night he was rather surprised at how quickly he consented to go along 'to hear Trevor and Esther again.'

Although he hadn't gone expecting anything dramatic to happen to him like what had happened to Claire in her first meeting, Ed heard more than Trevor and Esther that night. He heard the voice of God and opened his already softened heart to the Lord Jesus.

Now husband, wife and little son were all united in Christ.

Another couple, Dorothy and Wilfred Ross, had been coming regularly to the meetings in Tullygrawley, and one evening after a meeting Dorothy put her faith in the Lord Jesus Christ. When the mission came to an end, however, her husband Wilfred had shown little sign of any desire to be saved. Trevor and Esther were disappointed at this, for although they were thrilled at the number who had been converted they both had a special concern for Wilfred.

Spring gave way to summer and Trevor and Esther realised that the time was fast approaching when they would have to think of planning, and then packing, for the move to Cork. Before they went, though, there were a number of missions that had been arranged, and would have to be conducted. The last of these, prior to their move south, was to be held in Garvagh, County Londonderry, commencing on June 26, 1994.

This was to be a tent mission, and since it was the summer holiday Trevor and Esther were to be assisted by Jonathan Tink and David Lewis, two students from The Faith Mission Bible College, on mission placement. Part of their duty was to take care of the tent and they lived in a caravan in the field beside their canvas charge.

Active young men can often have healthy appetites and early in the second week David and Jonathan came to their mission leader with a problem.

"Trevor," they confided, "we have no jam. And we haven't had any for days."

"It's as the scriptures say, boys, 'You have not, because you ask not,'" Trevor replied with a smile. He then promised to ensure that they were provided with appropriate preserves the following day.

When he was speaking the next night Trevor was telling the people packed into the tent that God had provided them with salvation through the death of Christ on the cross of Calvary, and it was offered free to all those who would take it. Their problem, he informed them, was that they didn't have it simply because they didn't ask for it.

To illustrate his point he told them the story of David, Jonathan and the jam.

He had no idea what effect that story was going to have on the hard-working country women for miles around, many of whom were mothers with growing sons or treasured grandsons, however. Their hearts were touched, not so much by the spiritual plight of those who were constantly neglecting their soul's salvation, but by the physical plight of poor David and Jonathan who had no jam.

Next night the jam began to arrive. A steady stream of ladies called at the caravan on the way into the tent. They were presenting gooseberry jam, which had 'just been made today,' blackcurrant jam, which 'has such a clean, sharp taste' and strawberry jam which 'has always been my favourite.'

The boys were delighted with this influx of jam. When their collection was joined the following evening by rhubarb and ginger, Victoria plum, which was made from 'some plums I had in the freezer from last season,' and raspberry, which 'is so easy to make I just brought you a pot each,' however, David and Jonathan began to panic. The mission was going to have to last well into September or they were never going to be able to eat all their jam.

Trevor called in to see them on the third afternoon after his illustration and saw their dilemma. The tiny provisions cupboards in the caravan had long since ceased to be able to hold the jam. So the benches were lined with it and the two pots that were currently in use remained on the table for they had nowhere else to go.

There was only one way to stem the incoming tide of jam. That night as he was making a few announcements at the beginning of the meeting Trevor opened with what he said was 'a special message for all the good, kind women, of Garvagh and district.'

The eyes of all the ladies suddenly became focused on the platform, wondering what was coming next, when he began, "During this mission you have heard me make an occasional, earnest appeal at the end of a meeting. Tonight, though, I am making an earnest appeal at the beginning of this one."

Subdued laughter rippled around the tent when the preacher went on to beg, in all seriousness, "*Please, no more jam!*"

Trevor and Esther were delighted to see some of the people who had been regular supporters of the earlier mission in Tullygrawley coming along to the tent in Garvagh. Some of these friends were amongst the capacity crowd of around three hundred that attended on the final Sunday afternoon.

During the mission the inside perimeter of the tent had been lined with bales of straw, courtesy of a local farmer. The straw had been placed there as a draught excluder, to cut the cold around the feet of the listeners, on windy nights. On that last pack-out Sunday afternoon the bales of straw doubled as makeshift seating.

Esther was leading the meeting and was thrilled to notice, from the platform, that Dorothy and Wilfred from Tullygrawley were sitting on a bale of straw at the very back of the tent. When she had handed over to Trevor, who was to preach that afternoon, Esther went down and sat beside Wilfred.

As the meeting progressed she could sense that he was becoming more uneasy, and his restlessness wasn't caused by his uncomfortable seat. He could sense that the women on either side of him were praying for him while the message Trevor was delivering was stirring deep into his soul.

Before the close of the meeting Trevor felt he ought to make an appeal, and this time it would be far from frivolous. He said, "If anyone feels that God has been speaking to them, just raise your head, and Esther or I will be happy to have a word with you later."

The first person to raise his head was Wilfred. He had been waiting for this moment, so that he could get speaking to either of the husband and wife team, about salvation. Trevor read the scriptures and prayed with him, and Wilfred trusted the Saviour.

His conversion was significant for Trevor and Esther not only because of the burden they both had for him, nor for the fact that it represented another family circle complete in Christ, but also because he was the last person to be saved in their final mission before leaving the Magherafelt district.

During the second half of July Trevor and Esther began to make final preparations for their move, but they were also invited to a number of farewell meetings. These were happy occasions when they were reunited with so many people who had come to know the Lord over their three years of ministry in the area, but there were also many tears as their friends thought of them 'going so far away.'

Kathleen and Wray, who had been one of the first two couples to befriend them on their arrival in Magherafelt were not content just to bid them a sad 'goodbye' before they left, however. They insisted in coming along with the family in early August to help them settle into their new environment in Cork.

The Faith Mission had provided them with accommodation at the camp centre in Bandon, and Kathleen helped Esther add the 'woman's touch' that transformed it into a comfortable home. The boys were enrolled in a change of school before the start of the autumn term and Wray, who had many practical skills, undertook to help Trevor with some of the matters requiring immediate attention around their new surroundings.

As they looked at the camp centre, and recognised its potential, Trevor and Esther had a vision to see it modernised, and then utilised as a source of spiritual blessing to the young people of Ireland.

That was to be a long-term project, however. A more pressing problem for Trevor was the need of a study where he could store the library of Christian books he had accumulated since his Bible College days, and where he could be alone with God to prepare for his preaching and teaching ministry.

Wray set to work and within a fortnight he had transformed the garage into a comfortable study, much to Trevor's delight. He quipped that he had witnessed his first conversion since coming to Cork, although it was only that of a garage.

The big challenge lay up ahead. Could they refurbish the camp centre, and then see lives transformed from darkness to light, from sin to salvation and from the power of Satan to the peace of God, there?

28

YOU CAN'T QUENCH THIS MAN'S VISION!

In mid-September Trevor and Esther were visited, in their new location, by some of the senior figures in The Faith Mission. Dr. Colin Peckham, Willie Porter, and Alistair Patterson, who had all been in Cork to attend a valedictory service, called to see them.

Recognising the opportunity, with such a 'high-powered delegation' on site, to outline some suggestions for refurbishment, Trevor invited them to join him for a walk around the Camp Centre, before their meeting.

As they strolled around Trevor made full use of his chance to point out a number of improvements, which Esther and he felt that the Lord was directing them to make. These would, he contended, render the centre more user-friendly, and thus increase the numbers of young people who would be happy to come to it. This, in turn, could have the ultimate, and desired effect, of seeing such young people led to faith in Christ.

There were so many changes that Trevor and Esther proposed making for the better, and Trevor was so enthusiastic about these, explaining in some cases how he would envisage them being carried out, as the delegation walked around, that Willie Porter became apprehensive. Trevor gathered, from some of the comments he made, and some of the questions he asked about projected costs, that the Director of the Mission in Ireland had understandable reservations about the overall expenditure of such ambitious projects.

Dr. Peckham had become aware of the emergence of two different viewpoints as they walked around. On one hand there was Trevor's enthusiasm for the expansion of the work in the centre and on the other Willie's concerns about the financial burden the suggested improvements could create.

He remembered Trevor from Bible College and had obviously been impressed by his commitment to the work of the Lord as reflected in his zeal for the ideas he was putting forward. This became evident when he turned to Willie Porter at one stage and exclaimed, "Brother, you can't quench this man's vision!" Before Willie had even been given a chance to reply he went on to follow his opening declaration with an extremely welcome suggestion, "If you have any money give it to him!"

They continued their tour of the camp centre and as they did so Willie came to acknowledge the depth of Dr. Peckham's spiritual perception, and the wisdom of his advice. When they had seen all the various aspects of the camp centre and heard Trevor outline his long-term plan for them, Willie said to him, "We wouldn't want to quench your vision, Trevor." Then turning to Alistair Patterson, who was Superintendent of the South Irish District, he continued, "Give him five hundred pounds."

That initial donation was enough to allow materials to be purchased and work to begin on the centre straight away, and as soon as it began, offers of help began to flood in. Local tradesmen, and others who were willing to make the long trip from Northern Ireland, volunteered their services free of charge. These men occasionally became so engrossed in a particular job that they would work throughout the night to finish it.

With work continuing apace it soon became clear that the original gift wasn't going to prove sufficient to meet the mounting costs of the refurbishment. Trevor and Esther had been depending on the Lord to meet all their needs since they began serving Him, and He proved His faithfulness in this practical situation also. Although they never once made an appeal of any kind for funds, the money to cover all the building expenses began to pour in.

Local Christians, touched with Trevor and Esther's fervour for doing something significant for God in their area, donated large and small amounts. The dedicated couple appreciated all of these, accepting them as an indication of support and friendship.

One evening, after the Youth Fellowship meeting in Trevor and Esther's house, Hazel, one of the teenagers who had been present, gave them a bag of coins. "This is my tithe," she explained. "The Lord has told me that I am to give it to you and I would like you to use it for the work here in Cork." When all the five, ten, twenty and fifty pence coins were counted, Hazel's tithe, which she so willingly passed on, amounted to more than one hundred pounds.

On other separate occasions two local farmers each came to Trevor at different times and, totally unknown to each other, told him they felt that God was leading them to give him 'a gift towards the fixing-up of the camp centre.' They had come in response to that Divine prompting, and in each case their contribution was a cheque for one thousand pounds.

By the spring of 1995 the work had moved ahead by leaps and bounds. A new kitchen, dining room and games room had been built. Trevor and Esther then arranged an official opening of the revamped centre for the Saturday of the May Bank Holiday. Their aim in doing this was twofold. They wanted to allow others to join with them in praising God for His unfailing provision but they also considered it important to invite everyone who had helped with it, or donated to it, to see it complete.

There were, however, a number of jobs to be undertaken, before the centre was ready for such a 'big day.' The most pressing of these was the obtaining and then fitting of suitable modern units in the new kitchen, which was much larger than the previous one.

This need was met in an unexpected telephone call one day. Trevor, who was unable to be out working in the centre at the time because he was ill, took a call from Orrlee Kitchens in Magherafelt.

"I hear you could use a kitchen," the voice at the other end of the line began. "We have one here that has been ordered and not used and if you would like it, you can have it."

Trevor was taken aback at first. "But what if it doesn't fit?" he enquired. "Our new kitchen is quite big."

"Never you worry about that. If you send us up your measurements we will adapt it to your needs. We can supply you with enough units to fit out your kitchen," the caller assured him.

Having thanked him profusely, Trevor enlisted some of the local tradesmen to help him measure up the kitchen, and submit an outline plan of what units they would find most useful.

Orrlee did as they had promised and in a matter of weeks after receiving Trevor's plan they notified him to say that the kitchen was ready to be collected from their workshops. Trevor had friends in Drennan Transport of Tobermore and when he rang them and explained about the kitchen in Magherafelt that had to be moved to a Christian camp centre in Cork they offered to transport it free of charge.

Wray Ritchie and Archie Hogg from Northern Ireland travelled down to the centre to help the others already there with the installation of the brand new kitchen. When they had completed this work Archie realized that there was something more needed to be done to finish off the kitchen to everyone's satisfaction. Rather than talk about it, however, he undertook to supply all the floor and wall tiles, and tile the kitchen himself.

Thus the camp centre was totally revitalised on schedule, and more than three hundred people assembled on the day of the official opening to praise God for his amazing provision, and dedicate it to His glory.

In December 1994, when Trevor and Esther had begun to feel at home in Cork, and with the work in the camp centre progressing on schedule, and in fulfilment of their vision, they were to receive a nasty shock. The parents had been expecting to be charged for the boys' school fees and books but when the bills for them came in at the end of term they were taken aback. When these were all added together they amounted to more that five hundred pounds. This was an unexpected bombshell and an expense that they were not in a position to meet. How were they ever going to pay?

It had always been their experience that God was arranging to supply their need before they even knew they had it, and this case was no exception. He had impressed upon the heart of Jack Wylie, a farmer from outside Tobermore, to send them some financial assistance.

Jack's letter arrived with Trevor and Esther three days after the school bills and in it he said, 'I would like you to use this money for yourselves. Put it to what is your greatest need at the minute.' The grateful couple had no difficulty in identifying their 'greatest need,' and were thrilled to discover that with currency conversion from pounds sterling to Irish punts, it proved sufficient to cover the boys' school fees.

In acknowledging the gift Trevor and Esther told Jack that God had guided him both in the amount sent, and in the timing of it, for it had been enough to meet an immediate expense. They did not, however, tell him what that expense was.

What was perhaps even more astounding was that three times a year, for the duration of their stay in Cork, when the boys' school bills came in, a cheque from Jack arrived to cover them. He didn't know why he had fallen into a pattern of sending Trevor and Esther that particular amount at specific times of the year. God and his two humble, thankful servants did, though.

Trevor and Esther weren't long settled into the west Cork area until they embarked on a series of short missions, in addition to the work in the camp centre. One of these was held in Ballydehob Community Hall. The two speakers, who had been used to preaching to big crowds in many of their earlier missions, were slightly worried when only twelve people turned up on the opening night. As they continued calling at the homes in the area, however, they were more encouraged as numbers began to increase.

One of the most significant things to happen in that mission was that Sam and Hilda Attridge were restored to the joy of their salvation and a zeal for the work of God. Sam and Hilda had become cold in heart but when they had gone to hear Trevor and Esther preach they had experienced a genuine resurgence in their love for God and were possessed with a desire to do something for Him.

The mission that had begun so quietly ended on a high note. There were 160 people there on the closing night, and Sam and Hilda approached Trevor and Esther with a vision, which, they claimed, God had put into their hearts. They wondered if their new Christian friends and counsellors would come and preach at a series of 'cottage meetings' in their home, if they were to open it up for the Lord. There had never been Gospel meetings in the isolated area where they lived, as far as they could remember, and they would like their friends and neighbours to hear the message.

Trevor and Esther were delighted to be afforded this opportunity to preach in a new district and the mission held in Sam and Hilda's bungalow in Durrus in late 1997 proved to be one of the highlights of their ministry in the west Cork area up until then.

The hosts helped the speakers to invite their neighbours along and soon they were having difficulty in accommodating all who came, in their spacious bungalow. Trevor had brought chairs across from the camp centre and these were crammed into every available space and they were all needed. There were over a hundred people jammed into the house one evening. Trevor and Esther had just room to stand and speak in the hall, so that they could he heard in all the rooms.

God honoured Sam and Hilda's vision, too, for a number came to faith in Christ, including Sam's uncle. Nor did the blessing experienced in that mission end on its closing night, for a Fellowship Meeting was established in their home as a result of it.

With the modernisation of the camp centre the summer camp weeks proved to be a joy and delight. Trevor had always enjoyed working with the young people, but for Esther the work was in complete contrast to her earlier experiences where she had felt isolated and underused in the kitchen. She now worked away quite happily with the other willing volunteers, and the camps were soon to become very popular amongst the young people of the area.

Separate weekly camps were arranged for different age groups and by Trevor and Esther's second year in charge, these were oversubscribed, with long waiting lists. The centre was bursting at the seams, with enthusiastic, exuberant youngsters all summer long. God added His special blessing in those busy weeks too, with many children and young people committing their lives to the Lord Jesus.

Dr. Peckham had been right to warn against quenching 'this man's vision.'

29

REALITY

It was an unusual, but nonetheless welcome, invitation.

With the increasing activity level, occasional setbacks and endless responsibility of the work amongst the young people in the camp centre and out in missions all around west Cork, Trevor and Esther often became physically and mentally drained. They were, as one of their colleagues was heard to remark occasionally, 'not tired of the work, but often tired in it.'

The letter they had just received was inviting 'tired workers' to 'come apart and rest awhile.' The organisers were encouraging Christian workers who were giving themselves constantly and unstintingly to serving others in the service of the Lord, to come together for a weekend break. There they could meet a number of church and mission leaders who were in a similar situation, and share in a time of fellowship and refreshing ministry to their own souls. It had been arranged for a weekend in May 1997, the venue was to be

The Rock Centre in Portstewart, County Londonderry, and there would be, the invitation promised, a number of 'well-known guest speakers.'

Trevor and Esther found the prospect of such a weekend 'away from it all,' most appealing, and were more than ready to express their willingness to attend.

In one of the sessions over that weekend, Rev. Howard Lewis posed a number of thought-provoking questions in the course of his talk, which he had entitled, 'Reality.'

"Are you imprisoned in a situation?" he enquired.

"Are you doing the job God has gifted you for, or just a job that is there to be done?" he challenged.

"Are you having the same experience as Selwyn Hughes who discovered at one stage in his ministry that he was achieving only 'minimum effectiveness with maximum weariness?'" he asked.

Rev. Lewis was not to know how these questions were striking home to the hearts of the Faith Mission couple from Cork as he went on to follow what he imagined the responses to them would be, with a personal challenge.

"If these questions have struck a chord with some of you," he went on to confront the group bluntly, "why are you not doing something about it? How can you possibly remain in a situation knowing in your heart that it is not God's perfect plan for you? Are you afraid of letting others down? Afraid of failure, of letting yourself down, perhaps? Or could it be that you are afraid of what somebody might say about you? Surely it couldn't possibly be that you are afraid to step out and trust God...?"

In a break between meetings Trevor and Esther took a walk along the coastal path towards Portstewart promenade and as they did so Esther told her husband that God had been speaking to her during what Rev. Lewis had said. Trevor, who had been sitting across the room from his wife, as he had been later in arriving in the lounge for the meeting, confessed that the speaker's series of searching questions had caused him to ponder his own role as a servant of the Lord also.

As they strolled along in the late afternoon sunshine he told Esther that he had been wondering if it could be possible that although they were seeing encouraging things happening in Cork, God was now indicating that it was time to move on to another sphere of service. He was, he felt, called to be an itinerant evangelist, a Gospel preacher. Recalling their time in Magherafelt he remembered how God had blessed, and how fulfilled he had felt, when they had both been engaged in out-and-out evangelism.

Esther admitted to having felt exactly the same way, particularly over the previous year. Although the area and camp centre work was hugely rewarding she agreed with Trevor that their call from God was to be committed preachers of the Gospel.

These frank disclosures led to the couple who had come away for a break from the work in which they were involved in Cork, to seriously consider their future in it. They discussed Howard Lewis's point-blank challenge to the group to do something about the situation if they were convinced that God wanted them to serve Him in a more productive way, and applied it to themselves. Should they, for example, simply stay in Cork to save them the bother, or the embarrassment, of telling the leaders of The Faith Mission that they wanted to move?

By the time Trevor and Esther had returned to The Rock for tea they had come to a momentous decision. As soon as they arrived back in Cork they would write to the Mission and state their position.

The letter took some time to draft, for by sending it to the Mission Trevor and Esther knew that they could be ending their term with them, but they still felt it should be sent. They began by stating that they had come to realise 'more clearly as the days and months go by that area work is not our calling.' Having described how they had been challenged by 'the ministry of a dear brother on the theme of 'Reality,' they went on to state their belief that 'Trevor's gift' lay in evangelism.

They came to the crux of the matter when stating that 'we have no desire to leave The Faith Mission yet being realistic we understand that you may not have a place to keep us on.' Whether the Mission felt led' to keep them on as evangelists' or not Trevor and Esther felt that they 'could not remain in their present situation beyond the summer of 1998.'

Their expressed date for leaving Cork was still at least a year away, but Keith Percival didn't take that long to reply to the honest letter he had received from the area workers in Cork. His response came soon, and Trevor and Esther were most grateful for it.

'The Mission,' he wrote, 'recognised that Trevor's gift lay in evangelism, and had been expecting him to express this sentiment at some stage... Yes, most certainly there would be a place for them to operate as evangelists within the Mission family... They would see them relocated in the summer of 1998 at the latest...'

It was exciting news and Trevor and Esther both believed that although they were still seeing blessing in Cork the Mission's decision to keep them on confirmed their conviction that God was directing them to return to full-time evangelism.

A lot had now to be decided in the next twelve months. Where were they going to live? That was their first problem. Some had suggested that Belfast would make an ideal base from which to operate, but Trevor and Esther had reservations about this, for it would mean a total change of educational system for the boys. They had become accustomed to the 'southern' model and so a location somewhere in the Republic of Ireland would be more suitable from that point of view.

When Trevor was visiting his family in Monaghan a few weeks later he was sharing these thoughts with his brother Ronnie, who, as the oldest, had become accepted as a kind of 'father-figure' to the Gillanders family. They had chatted for a while in Ronnie's home when big brother suggested that they should go out for a walk.

They had walked up the hill from the farmhouse when Ronnie stopped at a gap in the hedge. He pointed into the field and said, "I have always thought that would make a great site for a house."

Trevor looked around him from where he was standing, for a moment. When he had surveyed the entire location he replied, "Aye. You're right, Ronnie. It would."

"That's O.K. then, Trevor," Ronnie said. "It's yours if you can see your way to build a house on it."

That was all that was said, but a seed was sown in Trevor's heart, and the more he began to water it with approval, the more it seemed to sprout and grow.

When he drove home to Cork and told Esther of Ronnie's offer, his wife just looked at him incredulously. "Lovely idea, Trevor," was her instinctive reaction, "but how? Building a house takes money, you know, and we don't have that kind of money."

"We could maybe arrange a mortgage," her husband said, not to be deterred.

"A mortgage," Esther repeated. "You are supposed to have a fixed income, and probably a good one at that to get a mortgage, as I understand it, Trevor. And as an evangelist you won't have a fixed income."

Although Esther was sceptical about the financial aspect of Trevor's suggestion she quite fancied the prospect of a move back to her home town. She helped him compile yet another letter to The Faith Mission, which this time contained an enquiry. It was, if they could obtain financial backing would the Mission have any objections to them building their own house in Monaghan?

The Mission approved this proposition since Monaghan would be an ideal location from which to reach out all over the Ireland, and so Trevor and Esther were free to go ahead with their plans.

Determined to fulfil his ambition of building a house on his brother's land, Trevor rang Eric Good, a Christian friend who was a mortgage adviser. He told Trevor to bring in his 'details' some day and he would tell him what was available.

When Trevor did as instructed, Eric examined the information he had before him intently for a minute of two before looking up to say, "You haven't a hope. They'll laugh at you, Trevor."

Trevor went home somewhat depressed. Maybe Esther had been right in the first place. That was only a man's assessment, however, he told himself later. If God wanted Esther and he to move to Monaghan, He would open the way for them.

His heart was set on the site in Monaghan, and on his next day off he drove north to his home town. He was, he told Esther, 'going to see how much Ronnie wanted for the site,' for both of them were determined to pay him market value for it, and 'to have a chat with the bank manager.'

When he arrived with his older brother he reminded him of their conversation some time earlier, and enquired how much he would sell the site to him for. Ronnie wasn't keen to put a price on it at all, but eventually agreed a compromise. "I tell you what, Trevor," he said at length. "I will give it to you at agricultural price, and you will only have to pay me when it suits you." He paused for a few seconds before adding, "And even if you were never to pay me it wouldn't matter."

After leaving Ronnie, Trevor called in with the manager in the National Irish Bank in the town, and this was to prove encouraging. When he had heard all Trevor had to say about his plans to return to the town, and about Ronnie and the site, the manager said, "We won't write you off, Trevor. Leave it with me and I will be in touch."

About a month later Trevor was out and Esther took a phone call from the bank manager. When Esther told him that her husband wasn't in he said, "Well, could you just tell him that his mortgage has been approved, and I will be in touch again."

This was an answer to prayer, for the main obstacle to building a house on the site in Monaghan had been removed. And God had not by any means finished providing for their move yet either.

On his way out of a meeting later that week Trevor was handed an envelope by one of the local Christians, who said, "God has been telling me for days that I should give that to you." When he opened it on arriving home, Trevor discovered that it contained enough money to give Ronnie what he had agreed would be 'agricultural value' for the site!

All that remained to be done then was to obtain planning permission and this was procured in record time, without any outward pressure or persuasion, and seemingly against all odds. It was unusual for permission to be granted on an initial application, without a frustrating series of setbacks.

Plans were drawn and approved and a builder commenced work on the house at the end of March, aware that Trevor and Esther were planning to move into it before the end of August. They were anxious to witness the construction of their new home, but couldn't because of their mission commitments in Cork. This meant that Trevor and Esther were in frequent contact with the builder by telephone, often more than once a day. Esther used to joke that theirs would be 'the first house ever to be built over the phone!'

When the news filtered out amongst their friends in 'the North' that Trevor and Esther were coming back to live much closer to them, they were delighted, and some chose to demonstrate their pleasure in practical ways. One of these was Jim Moffett, who with his wife Ruth had been such an encouragement to Trevor and Esther during their early days in Magherafelt.

Jim phoned the couple to Cork one day with an offer, soon after work had begun on the house. "I want to put the roof over your head," he said. "In other words, what I am telling you is, when the time comes I will provide the roof tiles for your new home."

During Trevor and Esther's final summer in Cork in 1998, the camp work was in full swing when Trevor was crippled with his bad back once again. The camps had been oversubscribed as usual and the first week with the juniors had proved a time of blessing. In the middle of the second week, which was the very active teenager's camp, however, Trevor woke up one morning in agony. He just couldn't move!

He was so disappointed, for he so much enjoyed the camp work, but his incapacity also meant that Esther and Gregory had to do all the packing and make all the arrangements for the move to Monaghan in August. Darren had already gone ahead of them to a summer job in the town.

The local Christians were disappointed, too, for they had arranged a special farewell meeting for the family, but Trevor was unable to attend. He tried to go, but when he had struggled from his bed into the shower, and then almost collapsed with the pain, he was glad to return to bed and forced to stay there.

His condition didn't improve, and on the day of the move he ended up lying in agony on a mattress in the middle of the floor, with everyone working around him. The bed had been dismantled to await the arrival of Ronnie, who had offered to act as furniture remover, with his small lorry. One of the last people to say 'Goodbye' to them before they left Cork was the doctor, who had called to give Trevor a pain-killing injection, before Esther drove him the 280 miles to their new home.

It seemed peculiar, with everything having gone so well in the camp work in Cork for four years, and with the building of the house in Monaghan over the past six months, that Trevor and Esther couldn't be permitted to effect a hassle-free transition between the two.

This, though, was reality.

30

YOU KEEP IGNORING ME

Trevor and Esther moved into rented accommodation in Monaghan after their move in mid - August 1998, and then into their new house during the first week in September.

Although they began with what they described as 'Axminster cardboard' on the floors God provided in a wonderful way for the fitting out of their new home over the next few months. Trevor's back gradually improved, and he was, by the time they had moved in, able to share in all the decisions that had to be made, and most of the work that had to be done.

One morning Trevor and Esther had gone into a shop in Monaghan to pick a fireplace. On their way in they spoke to a local Christian lady, who was sitting in her car in the yard.

It was almost half-an-hour later when Trevor and Esther emerged from the shop, and as they did so were somewhat surprised to find that the woman was still sitting in her car. Trevor crossed the road and had a short conversation with her. As he was turning to go back to join Esther in his own car, the lady said, "Trevor, this is for the both of you to help with the furnishing of your new house." Trevor and Esther were most grateful to God for the generous gift, which He had led the kind lady to pass across to them, and which went a long way to helping purchase the fireplace they had just chosen.

The pleasure that their new home brought to both of them was tinged with an occasional pang of conscience for Trevor. He always felt that his brother Ronnie hadn't been adequately reimbursed for the site on which it stood. Although he had given Ronnie his asking price Trevor was well away that if he had been buying it from someone else he would have been charged a lot more.

On contemplating this matter one day, Trevor prayed for his older brother. "Lord," he asked, "I can't repay Ronnie for his kindness to us, but please could You repay him with salvation." Ronnie's wife Joyce, and their daughters, were already Christians. It would be such a thrill for them all if he were to come to Christ.

One of Trevor's first missions on his return to his native district was in his home church, Ballyalbany Presbyterian. Ronnie, who was a member of the church, came almost every night to hear his younger brother speak. It brought great joy to both of them when Ronnie and Joyce came up to Trevor and Esther's home one evening in early December, after a meeting, to tell them that Ronnie had given his life to the Lord. Only then did Trevor tell him of his prayer that God would 'repay him with salvation.'

Months later Trevor and Esther were conducting a three-week mission in Clogh, near Rosslea in County Fermanagh. They were encouraged by the size of the audiences, with people both young and old from all around the area attending night after night.

One evening, when Trevor had chosen to speak on the subject of the second coming of Christ, he noticed that two young lads appeared particularly concerned. David and Berry Maxwell had been coming most nights with their parents, but on that night a singular sense of urgency seemed to have come upon them.

Realising that the two lads were not the only people in the meeting to have been paying rapt attention to the message, Trevor announced at the end of the meeting, "If God has been speaking to you in the meeting tonight and you would like to talk to us about salvation, please let us know. It doesn't matter where you live, or how far we have to travel, we would be happy to come and see you in the privacy of your home if we can help point you to the Saviour. Remember, this is an urgent matter."

Given the almost tangible sense of the presence of God that had been in the meeting Trevor was surprised, and not a little disappointed, that no one said anything more than 'Goodnight' to him on their way out of the hall.

He went home and was in bed sound asleep when he was awakened by the telephone in the early hours of the morning. When he answered it the voice at the other end of the line said, "Didn't you say that you would go anywhere at any time, Trevor, to speak to someone about salvation?"

"That's right," Trevor replied, suddenly wide-awake. "I did." This sounded promising

"This is Hugh Maxwell, David and Berry's father," the caller went on. " The two lads are both deeply concerned about their souls. They are both afraid to go to bed and go to sleep in case the Lord would return and they wouldn't be ready, They asked me to ring you. They said you would come over to see them."

"I most certainly will," the evangelist assured him without hesitation.

Trevor arrived at the Maxwell home half an hour later, and although it was by then well on into the night he found two very alert young lads waiting for him. It was clear that they weren't in the slightest bit interested in bed. All they were concerned about was knowing peace with God, and having the assurance that when the Lord came back they would be ready to meet Him.

Trevor began talking to the two lads, reading the Bible and praying with them. He soon discovered that their hearts were like what Jesus described in one of His parables as 'the good ground.' They had been thoroughly prepared by the Spirit of God and were ready to receive the seed of the Gospel, and produce a harvest of salvation. In a very short time both David and Berry had come simply to faith in

Christ.

It was a joy to Trevor to see the transformation that came over those lads' faces. From being very worried-looking, almost fear-stricken, they were suddenly happy, shining and relaxed. The change that had taken place in their hearts had immediately registered on their countenances.

Little did Trevor know but when he was in the room counselling her two sons their mum had been preparing a meal, a real middle of the night feast, for them all. Trevor couldn't really determine whether it was intended to be a very late supper or a very early breakfast, but it didn't really matter. Whatever it was there was a wonderful sense of peace and thanksgiving around the table as everyone praised the Lord for His goodness.

It was a long trip from Monaghan to Magherally outside Banbridge, in County Down, yet Trevor and Esther did it happily, for Trevor to conduct a mission there. It is very encouraging for a speaker to see a hall well filled with attentive listeners, and that's how it was in Magherally.

The regular attendance of the Irvine family of eight, father, mother and six children was always a boost to the numbers and an inspiration to the preacher. The children, and especially Stephen, were so enthusiastic during the chorus singing before the meeting that their fervour was infectious.

When Trevor asked for 'a favourite' from his congregation in the community singing each evening Stephen was constantly asking for,

'Let the Lord have His way,
In your life every day...'

The young lad would then proceed to sing this chorus with great gusto, looking perfectly happy. This led Trevor and Esther to assume that he was one of the more outgoing members of a lovely Christian family who constantly came along en bloc to support them.

As the mission progressed Trevor made an appeal on a number of nights. He did this by inviting those who were interested in getting saved, to raise their heads, so that he could identify them for counselling. When Stephen lifted his head on a number of occasions, Trevor thought that it was merely out of a sense of boyish curiosity to see what was going on.

One other night Trevor announced at the end of a particularly solemn service, "If you would like us to call and see you in home some time, just speak to either of us at the door." Stephen asked him that night to 'come round and see him sometime', but again Trevor thought that this was nothing more than an attention-seeking desire to have the preacher call at his home. As he didn't have time for cosy chats in Christian homes, with so many non-Christians to be visited, Trevor deferred making a call on Stephen.

Finally, one evening, Stephen became quite determined that he wasn't going to be fobbed off any longer. Before leaving the hall he looked the preacher straight in the eye and begged, "Trevor, will you please come and see me soon!" Sensing that the lad was in earnest about something, and reckoning that it could do no harm to call with him for ten or twenty minutes, Trevor agreed to pay him a visit the following afternoon.

When Trevor arrived at the home he discovered Stephen and his brother Alan eagerly expecting him. Stephen had been instrumental in arranging this visit, and it was he who opened the conversation. "I am glad to see you here at last," he began, in a tone that echoed both mild exasperation and eventual satisfaction. "I have been raising my head in the meetings for ages and you keep ignoring me. I asked you to come and see me before and you never bothered. Now you are here, I want to be saved!"

His brother Alan also expressed a desire to come to faith in Christ and before Trevor left that home he had seen another two lads accept the Lord Jesus into their hearts. Their mum and dad were thrilled to hear this, and they were absolutely overjoyed when the boys' sister Emma also came to know the Lord a short time later.

Trevor reckoned that he had learnt a lesson from Stephen, and God chose to emphasise the importance of his personal calling to him, through Michelle.

When he was conducting a mission in Ardress Mission Hall, in County Armagh, Michelle, who was disabled and confined to a wheelchair, began to attend regularly with her parents.

About the middle of the second week, Trevor and Esther both

noticed that the Mc Cann family appeared very interested in the messages being preached and seemed concerned about spiritual matters. When the preachers were conscious of this occurring during meetings they often decided to pay such people a visit to afford them the opportunity to air their anxieties in conversation.

On the afternoon when they called Michelle and her mother, Edith, were together in the house. They needed no prompting. It was as though they had been waiting for Trevor and Esther to call with them and they immediately began to talk about their need to be saved.

That afternoon, before they left the Mc Cann home, Trevor and Esther saw both mother and daughter put their faith in the Lord Jesus Christ for salvation. It was soon evident, also, that everything had changed in their lives, but Michelle's attitude was an extra special joy to witness. Although disabled, her pure love for the Lord, her constant encouragement to others, whatever their circumstances, and her unfailing attendance at and enthusiastic appreciation of, every meeting, was to make her an inspirational figure around Ardress Mission Hall, in the coming months.

The challenge for Trevor came when, less that two years after that joyful afternoon when she was saved, Michelle went into hospital for what was expected to be routine surgery. Complications developed, however, and within hours Michelle had passed away.

On hearing of her sudden call home to her undoubted reward in heaven, Trevor was struck immediately by two totally contrasting reactions. The first was that it is 'happy for Michelle' because she had been prepared to die and had gone 'to be Christ, which is far better.'

The other was to have more of a lasting impact upon his ministry.

He determined to preach even more earnestly, leaving nobody in any doubt, not only about the urgency and importance of coming to Christ for salvation, but also about the satisfaction and assurance that such a commitment affords.

31

ON A MISSION TO A MISSION

Trevor and Esther were now happily engaged in what they believed God had called them to do, and blessing seemed to follow them, most places they went. They travelled the length and breadth of Ireland from their new home in Monaghan, and in places as far apart as Kilkenny and Kilrea, or Ballymacbrennan and Ballymoney, they witnessed people of all ages brought into a vibrant and eternal relationship with Jesus Christ.

There were rare occasions in their ministry, however, when something unexpected, and even puzzling, occurred. An example of this happened when they were conducting a mission in Boveedy, outside Kilrea, County Londonderry, in March 2000.

Big crowds of people from the district were attending every night and on the evening they had invited the Coagh Christian Fellowship along to sing they expected it to be a pack-out. It was, and the unanticipated arrival of three car-loads from Larne Mission Hall rendered the hall crammed to the point that some of those crushed into insufficient space began to feel uncomfortable.

The 'Coagh Boys,' as Trevor and Esther had come to know them affectionately, sang with great feeling. Trevor chose as his text, Hebrews 2 v. 3, 'How shall we escape, if we neglect so great salvation?' and preached with great fervour. The Larne delegation left after a brief period of sincere head-nodding and friendly hand-shaking during which they testified to having felt 'a real sense of the presence of God in that meeting.'

Why, though, had they come, so many of them, so far? Trevor wondered on his way back home in the car. Perhaps they wanted to book the Coagh Christian Fellowship for one of their meetings. Or maybe it was some kind of a church outing. Or perhaps... He just didn't know, so he would just have to forget it, for the present at least. There were so many different things to attend to, and so many other missions coming up.

One of these was a summer tent mission in their home town. Many of the local Christians, having heard of the remarkable way in which God was working in Trevor and Esther's missions all over the country, asked them to consider an evangelical outreach in Monaghan, assuring them of their full support.

The couple approached this mission with a certain degree of trepidation, remembering the words of their Master about His less than enthusiastic reception on returning to Nazareth. He declared, 'A prophet is not without honour except in his own country, among his own relatives and in his own house.'

They needn't have worried, however.

Those who promised to support them did so unreservedly, and from the opening night it was clear that this was going to be an exceptional mission. The crowds attending were so phenomenal that by the start of the second week they had to add two additional sections to the end of the tent and even then, with a seating capacity of over five hundred, it didn't accommodate all the people. Those who came included an unusually, but encouragingly, high percentage of young people, and all were happy to find somewhere to sit within earshot of the speaker, even if it was on the grass outside, on the warm, dry evenings.

At the close of one particular meeting at which Esther had

preached, three men came out of the tent one after another and they could barely speak to her at the door. Esther could sense that all of them were being mightily challenged by the Spirit of God. One of the three was Ivor Lowey, who drove home in a daze of spiritual anguish. It was only when his father arrived home from the tent, having been offered a lift by someone else, that Ivor became aware of his oversight. He had been so taken up worrying about his sin, his soul and his salvation that he had left his dad behind!

Ivor worked in the Heinz food factory in Dundalk and it was normally a rather noisy workplace. For the next couple of days, though, the rattle and whirr of the machinery was drowned out by the all prevailing voice of God, speaking to his soul.

Having been on the early shift on the second day after having been so moved during Esther's message Ivor decided that he would return home early. It had been pay day and he wanted to be back to the bank in Monaghan in time to lodge his pay cheque before closing time.

As he drove along the wide, open Dublin Road that led into the town he felt God speaking powerfully to him. 'Ivor,' He said, 'you are on the broad road, and it leads to destruction. You need to get onto the narrow road that leads to life…'

Just with that he saw the end of an actual narrow road coming up ahead. And it was the road on which Trevor and Esther lived! Then God spoke again. 'See that narrow road. That's where the preacher lives, and that's the road you need to be on…'

Ivor turned into it without even thinking. It was as though his car had suddenly become dual-controlled and an unseen instructor had taken over the steering-wheel. As he drove along that road he met Trevor and Gregory coming the opposite direction. Trevor recognised Ivor's car and stopped, only to find the young man in floods of tears. The experienced evangelist didn't even have to ask him what was wrong. He knew instantly that Ivor was in spiritual turmoil.

Trevor considered that Ivor was not fit to be in control of a vehicle so he drove his car back to their house, with Gregory following behind in the one he and his dad had set out in. There were other friends in the house when the trio arrived back, somewhat to Esther's surprise, but Trevor just told her how they had met Ivor on the road and that they were going into the study.

They weren't long in there either until Ivor saw that Christ had died on the cross to take the punishment for all those sins that had been so perplexing him over the past few days, and accepted Him simply as his Saviour.

He was soon back up with the others, his eyes still red where he had been weeping, but his mouth praising God for salvation. "I've got saved! I've got saved!" was all he could exclaim in joy and wonder, to everyone in the house in turn.

One morning just after Ivor's conversion Trevor was speaking on the telephone to Sam Condell, a leading Christian in the Monaghan area. They were discussing the progress of the mission and recounting the stories of those who had just recently trusted the Lord.

Sam went on to talk about some of those who were still attending regularly, and for whom they were still praying earnestly. Amongst those he mentioned were Jim and Thelma Dixon, and as soon as Trevor heard their names the Lord impressed it on his heart to go and see them at once.

Thelma showed Trevor into the living room after he had arrived at her house and greeted him with the words, "It's great to see you Trevor. I have been praying all morning that the Lord would send you here, so I'm not really surprised that you have called." She then asked to be excused for a moment until she called Jimmy in 'from the yard,' for both of them wanted to speak to him.

When all three of them were together, Jimmy and Thelma told Trevor that since they had begun to attend the mission regularly they had talked to each other a lot about getting saved. They were pleased to have him there to tell them more about it, they said.

Trevor read a number of different Bible passages with them, explaining from them, as simply as he could, how that God had provided free salvation for sinful mankind through the death of His Son. The couple were extremely interested in what he had to say and asked a number of intelligent, and relevant questions.

This continued for some time until Trevor decided to call a halt. "We can talk from now until the cows come home," he said. "What God requires is not talk though, it is action. He is calling you to come to Him. Now. Here. This morning."

That ultimatum stirred the young couple into action, and as they all knelt down on the living room floor, Trevor prayed and then Jimmy and Thelma prayed, and as they did so opened their hearts to the Saviour.

In that same summer following the mission in Monaghan, the tent was moved to Darragh Cross, near Downpatrick, in County Down. Although this was a new area, with different people attending, it represented the same challenge. That was seeing the men, women and children of the district reached with the message of the Gospel.

Hard on the heels of the spiritual fulfilment of seeing so many lives touched in Monaghan, Trevor and Esther found the first week and a half in Darragh Cross tough going for a number of reasons. The local Christians were very supportive, and indeed one of them, Ian Jackson, allowed them to stay over in his home for the duration of the mission. Despite their interest, however, Trevor and Esther considered it unusual, and disappointing, that they weren't experiencing the power of God in their preaching, and His blessing in salvation, in the way they had come to expect. It was as though some unseen evil influence was set to thwart them at every turn.

Then, in the middle of the second week everything changed. Suddenly it seemed as if the cold tap had been switched off and the hot switched on. That was when Trevor, Esther and Joel Luscher from Switzerland, were joined on the team by Simon Walsh from Northern Ireland. Joel and Simon were both students at the Faith Mission Bible College and were engaged in a programme of summer work. These two young men were helpful, enthusiastic, and extremely keen to work alongside their mentors in visitation and the outreach to children.

Soon the blessing that they so much missed began to become evident in the meetings. Crowds started to gravitate towards the tent, and during the third week the sides of the tent had to be lowered when it was full to capacity, to allow people sitting outside or in their cars to see and hear. On cooler evenings, when sitting outside would not be possible, and with no room in the field near the tent for cars, some people had no option but to turn and go home. Christians from many parts of County Down caught the vision, too, and soon the prayer caravan was jam-packed with them, all anxious to pray for the mission.

With this upturn in crowd numbers and an increased expectation in prayer there came a singular buzz of spiritual excitement about the mission, with many people from all age groups coming to Christ.

It was in the midst of times such as these, when God seemed to be stamping His seal of approval on their work as itinerant evangelists, that Trevor and Esther were called upon to make a crucial decision. They knew that it had long implications for both their ministry and their life style, and so were forced to give it careful, and prayerful consideration.

In the autumn of 2001 it became evident that the three carloads that had travelled from Larne to Boveedy well over a year before, hadn't just been there for the night out. They had come to a mission on a mission. It was clear that they had been what could be loosely described as 'a hearing committee,' for the leadership of Larne Mission Hall approached Trevor that September to ask him if he would consider becoming a full-time pastor with them. They had, they said, been struck by the manifest power of God in Boveedy, and had heard nothing but encouraging reports of his ministry since, and so had felt that they should make this approach and offer.

Trevor found it gratifying to be so highly thought of by such godly men as these, but their offer gave him a lot to think about.

Had he and Esther not considered themselves evangelists, first of all?

They had seen great blessing on the road, going from town to town, preaching the good news of salvation. Would they be expected to give that up, and if they were, would they be happy to take that step? On the other hand settling in an area and working with the same group of people in a pastoral role and building up relationships with them could surely have its merits too…?

Trevor played for time in the long run. He was booked to conduct a mission in the Larne hall in November, so he said, " To be fair to the mission, I think it would be better to wait until it is over. Then I will give your proposal serious and prayerful consideration."

32

THE WEE WOODEN HUT

The evident enthusiasm of the Christians in Larne Mission Hall for the work of the Lord, during the successful Gospel campaign in November only served to heighten Trevor's sense of indecision about the future. He had begun to ask God for guidance in relation to the overtures from Larne, but none seemed to be forthcoming.

This left him wavering.

On some days the prospect of a resident pastorate appealed to him.

Then the next day he had changed his mind. Had he not been called to 'do the work of an evangelist?'

Finding himself unable to make a definite decision on the matter, he contacted the elders in Larne Mission Hall in the early weeks of 2002 and explained to them that it had always been his policy not to make a move until he felt clearly that it was God's will for him to do so. Since he was still uncertain about going to Larne he felt compelled to say 'No', at least in the meantime.

The leaders of the Larne church were not so ambivalent, however. They believed that Trevor was God's man for them, and asked him to reconsider his decision. The busy preacher agreed to do so, but set a deadline. He told the anticipative, but not pushing, elders that he would give them a final and definite answer in the week before Easter.

That left him with two months in which to make up his mind one way or another. Trevor and Esther talked about it from time to time, and both of them, realising that whatever decision they made could have long-term implications for the life and ministry of each of them, prayed earnestly about it.

One night, when Esther was conscious that Trevor hadn't mentioned the 'Larne issue' for some time, as though he were trying to forget about it, and hope it would go away, she asked him, "What are you going to do about the call to Larne Mission Hall, Trevor? Why are you not accepting it?"

This pointed enquiry demanded an honest answer, and it was then that Trevor shared one of the matters that still remained unresolved in his mind, with his wife. It had been causing him constant concern ever since the first approach had been made, but he had never felt that the right time had come to voice it.

That moment had arrived now, though, so he looked across at Esther, who was sitting, wondering what was taking him so long to give her a simple answer. "There is no way that I could ask you to leave this house, Esther. You have put so much into it, and I know it means a lot to you," he told her.

It was now Esther's turn to respond, but she had no hesitation in giving her reply to her husband's kind consideration of her feelings. She had suspected for some time that expecting her to leave the home in Monaghan, which had by then been decorated and furnished to her personal desire and design, might be a sticking point with her husband. So she had her answer ready.

Fixing Trevor in a loving gaze she replied, "When we were building this house I told the Lord that if it ever became a noose around our necks in His service to burn it down. I would never want it, or indeed anything else, to stand in the way of us being in the will of God. Please forget about that. I will be happy to go where you go, provided we are both convinced that it is what He has had planned for us."

With that subject having been satisfactorily resolved Trevor was in his study the next morning, preparing to lead a Bible study on 2 Timothy chapter two. As he opened the Bible to commence his preparation he glanced down the opening verses of chapter four. The fifth verse contained the exhortation, which he had been using to create a case for remaining in Monaghan, and carrying on as he had been for the previous four years. It was, 'do the work of an evangelist.'

Suddenly, however, the next phrase, which he had up until then chosen to ignore as being somehow less significant, seemed to jump off the page at him.

'Make full proof of your ministry,' it counselled.

Trevor sat spellbound for a few minutes, contemplating what this could mean, not so much for Timothy as for him. He read it over again a time or two and then called out, "Esther, come in here to you see this."

When his wife joined him he was sitting with his Bible open and his eyes shining as though he had just received an unexpected, but pleasant, surprise. "Look," he began, eagerly. "I was just looking at that verse we often quote from second Timothy, 'do the work of an evangelist.' That was when I noticed the next bit where it goes on to say, 'make full proof of your ministry,' or 'fulfil your ministry,' is what it says here may be a more accurate translation."

Before waiting for any reaction from Esther he went on, "That has settled it for me. I have to move to engage in fulfilling a more complete ministry, which could include not only evangelism, but also scriptural teaching and pastoral visitation as well. I am going to ring Larne Mission Hall sometime soon and tell them we are coming."

Later that evening, as they were discussing what they should do next, or even first, Trevor confessed to still feeling in a bit of a dilemma. "You know, Esther, " he said, "for the past few months I have been saying 'No' to Larne, when I wanted to say 'Yes.' And now that God has clearly told me to say 'Yes', my natural reaction is to say

'No!"

There was to be no turning back, however. The next afternoon he phoned Tommy Campbell from Larne Mission Hall and told him that he believed the Lord was clearly guiding him to take up their call. The reaction was one of gratitude to God for 'a definite answer to prayer,' and a meeting was arranged to discuss the details of the appointment.

At that meeting Trevor told a committee from the Hall that he had a number of missions arranged and felt he should fulfil these bookings. The men from Larne were very happy for him to honour all his prearranged commitments, whether before or after the date set for him to take up his pastorate with them. It was also agreed that when he assumed the role of pastor in their Hall he should not completely cease to 'do the work of an evangelist,' but would be free to conduct missions elsewhere on a limited basis, and with the full support of his new church.

After some discussion of the issues concerned on both sides it was arranged that Trevor would assume the role of pastor in Larne Mission Hall in January 2003. Esther decided that she would like to remain in Monaghan until June to allow Gregory to finish his secondary education in the local school, before coming to live permanently in the County Antrim town.

Before, and immediately after embarking upon this new phase of their ministry, Trevor and Esther continued to conduct the different missions that had already been planned, and God continued to bless in many ways.

At Lismacarroll Mission Hall in Drumahoe, near Londonderry, people were queuing up to gain admission long before the hall was even open. One of the most notable aspects of that mission for Trevor and Esther was the number of children who came. These young people not only attended the children's activities but came also to the main meetings where they sat in rapt, reverent rows, listening to the message.

It was one of those campaigns with such a sense of spiritual awareness and expectation about it that Trevor and Esther could hardly wait from one night to the next to get there. Many people, both young and old, came to faith in Christ during what some dared to describe as that 'mini-revival' in Lismacarroll. There were so many, indeed, that when Tuesday evening discipleship classes were established in the wake of the mission more that sixty people came each night.

There was another mission, too, during which Trevor and Esther experienced the presence and blessing of the Lord in a particular way, and this in turned served to confirm to them that the decision to take up the pastorate in Larne had been right. This was their time in Lurganearly, a small Mission Hall in County Monaghan.

All but a few of the organisers had left the hall one evening when a lady who had been in the meeting, returned, and asked to speak to Esther. Her name, she said, was Kelly Ann and one of the local Christians had offered to baby-sit and that was why she and her husband, Nigel, had been in the meeting. She then went on to say that what she had heard in the meeting had affected her so much that she didn't want to go home until she had made her peace with God.

At that point Trevor had joined his wife and Kelly Ann and this was the kind of confession that was music to their ears. They both talked to her and within half-an-hour they had pointed her to the Lord for salvation. Kelly Ann was one of many who came to faith in Christ during that mission, but when it ended Nigel remained apparently unaffected.

A short time later Trevor had a phone call from his sister Caroline who is a Christian, and was then nursing on the coronary care ward in Monaghan General Hospital. "Nigel, who went to your mission in Lurganearly is in the coronary ward on a monitor," she told him. "His wife Kelly Ann is very concerned about him."

Trevor and Esther made a trip to the hospital to visit Nigel the next day, and when speaking to him emphasised his need of salvation. They did not, however, labour the subject as they realised that Nigel was in a precarious state of health.

When Kelly Ann arrived in to see her husband later on that evening she found him very disturbed. It wasn't his physical heart condition he was worried about though, it was his spiritual heart condition. He told his wife that he wanted to know the peace and joy in life that she had found. Kelly Ann was both overcome and overjoyed to hear this, and the woman who had only been a Christian little more than a week herself explained the Gospel in very simple terms and Nigel opened his troubled spiritual heart to the Saviour.

That night Trevor received a very excited call from Monaghan General Hospital. Caroline had brought a mobile phone unit to Nigel's bedside so that he could 'confess with his mouth the Lord Jesus,' to her delighted brother.

Late in 2002 when the Christians from Monaghan and district began to realise that the time was fast approaching when Trevor and Esther would be leaving them to take up their new challenge in Larne, they began to call to wish them every blessing. One of those who called one afternoon was Jack Wylie, the man who had been so faithful in his support of the Gillanders family for the previous seven years.

Trevor was out at the time and as Esther and Jack sat talking over a cup of tea Esther said to their gracious benefactor, "Jack, did you ever wonder what we did with all that money you so sent us so faithfully?"

"Yes," Jack replied quietly, "I suppose I did, but I never questioned it. All I know is that God kept telling me to send a certain amount at regular intervals and from the letters I got back from you, it always seemed to be useful."

"It wasn't just useful, it was vital, Jack," Esther went on. "Those regular intervals you talk about were always the end of a school term when we had school fees coming in."

She paused a moment to look across at the good-hearted farmer, where he was sitting on the sofa, before delivering her punch line, which was, "Little did you know it, Jack, but God has been using you to put our two sons through school."

Esther was not surprised to see a tear well up in Jack's eye when she told him this. He was deeply moved. So that was why he had felt so compelled to send Trevor and Esther money all down the years.

Jack was one of those invited, along with hundreds of others, both of family and friends, to Trevor's induction service in Larne Mission Hall on Saturday, January 18, 2003. As cars converged on the east Antrim town from many parts of Ireland, some of their occupants, and amongst them one or two of Trevor and Esther's relatives from

Monaghan, expressed their hitherto secret reservations about the wisdom of the couple 'tying themselves down to preaching in one little hall.'

What a surprise was in store for them when they arrived, however. They were astonished to find a large, modern building with a huge car park that was fast filling up. And if they were surprised when they saw the outside of Larne Mission Hall they were totally bowled over when stepped into it.

Trevor and Esther were moving around in the vast entrance lobby to greet their invited, but already dumbfounded, guests, and as they did so they were to hear, again and again, "Isn't this a beautiful place! It's not at all like we imagined! We thought we were coming to some wee wooden hut in the corner of a field!"

When the guests moved on through into the main sanctuary they found that it was also extremely spacious and modern, whilst maintaining, at the same time, an unmistakeable aura of reverence and respect. Attractive floral arrangements added a touch of colour to the scene and lively Christian music created a joyous, expectant atmosphere.

Those who had come in what they considered 'good time, for the service, found themselves standing around, waiting to be seated, and by the time the stewards had found a place for everyone, there were nearly seven hundred people in the building. They were everywhere, either crammed into the main body of the church, or sitting on chairs in the large minor hall or in the lobby.

There was such a jubilant, thankful atmosphere in the service as the leadership of the church told of the thrill it was for them to welcome Trevor as their pastor.

As her husband stood up to formally accept the pastorate of the church, Esther who was sitting with her two sons Darren and Gregory in the front row, looked up at him with a lump in her throat. She was so proud of him, so happy to be his wife.

It was strange, but as she watched Trevor, up high on the platform, and listened to what he had to say, she had a sudden flashback to another unforgettable picture of him.

That, too, had been a January afternoon, twenty years before, almost to the day.

The church had been packed to overflowing then, as well.

The difference, though, was that the poignant memory she suddenly recalled of Trevor, on that afternoon, was of him stumbling out of the church, in a grief-stricken stupor. Tears were streaming down his face. He was carrying a tiny urn, draped in a blue cloth.

As she contemplated that scene, David Hillen's words echoed in her ears.

'A little child shall lead them, ' he had predicted.

It had proved so true.

God had used their little 'Monty' to lead them so very, very far.